Audun and the Polar Bear

Medieval Law and Its Practice

VOLUME 1

Audun and the Polar Bear

Luck, Law, and Largesse in a Medieval Tale of Risky Business

By

William Ian Miller

BRILL

LEIDEN • BOSTON
2008

Cover illustrations: Fols. 206r. and fol. 206v. from GKS 1005: Flateyjarbók. With kind permission of the Árni Magnússon Institute for Icelandic Studies, Reykjavík.

Background cover illustration: Details from folio 69v., Balliol College MS. 350. The copyright of the background cover image belongs to Balliol College, Oxford, England, and no reproduction may be made without written permission.

This book is printed on acid-free paper.

Library of Congress Cataloging-in-Publication-Data

Auðunar þáttr vestfirzka. English
Audun and the polar bear : luck, law, and largesse in a medieval tale of risky business / by William I. Miller.
p. cm. — (Medieval law and its practice, ISSN 1873-8176 ; v. 1)
Includes bibliographical references.
ISBN 978-90-04-16811-4 (hardback : alk. paper) 1. Auðunar þáttr vestfirzka. 2. Law, Scandinavian—Sources. 3. Sagas. I. Miller, William Ian, 1946– II. Title. III. Series.

PT7288.A8E5 2008
839'.63—dc22 2008014093

ISSN 1873-8176
ISBN 978 90 04 16811 4

PRINTED IN THE NETHERLANDS

CONTENTS

PART ONE

THE CLOSE COMMENTARY

PART TWO

EXTENDED THEMES

ACKNOWLEDGMENTS

In accordance with the themes of this book I wish to express gratitude as some small payback for favors received: to John Crigler, Don Herzog, John Hudson, Kathleen Koehler, and Peter Potter for reading the entire manuscript and saving me from some, only some, of my usual excesses; to Kari Gade, Brian Simpson, Katja Škrubej, and Svanhildur Óskarsdóttir, for particular points of value. I wish too to thank the Carnegie Centenary Trust for an honorary professorship that funded a half year at the University of St. Andrews where the pleasures of conversation with the members of its sans pareil Department of Medieval History rekindled my interest in Norse matters, leading me to set aside, for the time being at least, forays into humiliation, pretense, disgust, courage, and body parts and getting me back instead to the texts I love best.

I wish to dedicate this essay to my students, law-students at that, past, present, and still to come in my ever-shortening future.

Ann Arbor, 2008

ABBREVIATIONS

Algazi, et al.	Gadi Algazi, Valentin Groebner, and Bernhard Jussen, eds., *Negotiating the Gift: Pre-Modern Figurations of Exchange*, Veröffentlichungen des Max-Planck-Instituts für Geschichte, 188 (Göttingen, 2003).
Andersson and Gade	Theodore M. Andersson and Kari Ellen Gade, trans. and commentary, *Morkinskinna: The Earliest Icelandic Chronicle of the Norwegian Kings (1030–1157)*, Islandica 51 (Ithaca, NY, 2000).
CSI	*The Complete Sagas of Icelanders including 49 tales*, ed. Viðar Hreinsson, 5 vols (Reykjavík, 1997).
F	*Flateyjarbók: en samling af norske konge-sagaer med indskudte mindre fortællinger om begivenheder i og udenfor Norge samt annaler*, 3 vols, ed. Guðbrandur Vigfússon and C.R. Unger (Christiania [Oslo], 1860–1868). *Audun's Story* at 3:411–415.
Grágás	*Grágás: Islændernes lovbog i fristatens tid*, 3 vols, ed. Vilhjálmur Finsen (Copenhagen, 1852–1883; rpt. Odense, 1974); (Konungsbók, vol. 1), (Staðarhólsbók, vol. 2), (Skálholtsbók and fragments, vol. 3). There is a superb translation of Konungsbók with selections from Staðarhólsbók and other mss: *Laws of Early Iceland: Grágás. The Codex Regius of Grágás with Material from other Manuscripts*, 2 vols, trans. Andrew Dennis, Peter Foote, and Richard Perkins (Winnipeg, 1980, 2000). Vol. 1 contains *Grágás* Ia 1–Ia 217; vol. 2, *Grágás* Ia 218–Ib 218 in Finsen's pagination. I follow the conventional practice of citing to volume number in Roman and page number in Finsen's pagination.

H The Hulda ms. version of *Audun's Story*, in *Fornmanna Sögur*, ed. Sveinbjörn Egilsson, et al., 12 vols (Copenhagen, 1825–1837), 6:297–307.

ÍF *Íslenzk Fornrit* (Reykjavík, 1933–). This series is the standard edition of the sagas, not yet including *Sturlunga saga*.

ÍF 1. *Landnámabók*, ed. Jakob Benedicktsson, 1968.

ÍF 2. *Egils saga Skalla-Grímssonar*, ed. Sigurður Nordal, 1933.

ÍF 3. *Borgfirðinga sögur*, ed. Sigurður Nordal and Guðni Jónsson, 1938. Includes *Bjarnar saga Hítdælakappa.*

ÍF 4. *Eyrbyggja saga*, ed. Einar Ól. Sveinsson and Matthías Þórðarson, 1935. Includes *Brands þáttr örvi.*

ÍF 5. *Laxdæla saga*, ed. Einar Ól. Sveinsson, 1934. Includes *Halldórs þáttr Snorrasonar.*

ÍF 6. *Vestfirðinga sögur*, ed. Björn K. Þórólfsson and Guðni Jónsson, 1943. Includes *Fóstbræðra saga, Þorvarðar þáttr krákunefs* and the M version of *Auðunar þáttr*.

ÍF 8. *Vatnsdæla saga*, ed. Einar Ól. Sveinsson, 1939. Also includes *Hallfreðar saga.*

ÍF 9. *Eyfirðinga sögur*, ed. Jonas Kristjánsson, 1956. Includes *Sneglu-Halla þáttr, Þorgríms þáttr Hallasonar.*

ÍF 10. *Ljósvetninga saga*, ed. Björn Sigfússon, 1940. Also includes *Hreiðars þáttr.*

ÍF 11. *Austfirðinga sögur*, ed. Jón Jóhannesson, 1950. Includes *Ásu-Þórðar þáttr, Vápnfirðinga saga, Þorsteins þáttr austfirðings.*

ÍF 12. *Brennu-Njáls saga*, ed. Einar Ól. Sveinsson, 1954.

ÍF 16. *Biskupa sögur*, vol. 2, ed. Ásdís Egilsdóttir, 2002. Includes *Hungrvaka* and *Ísleifs þáttr byskups.*

ÍF 26. *Heimskringla*, vol. 1, ed. Bjarni Aðalbjarnarson, 3rd ed., 1979; *Óláfs saga Tryggvasonar*, pp. 225–372.

ÍF 28. *Heimskringla*, vol. 3; *Haralds saga Sigurðarsonar*, pp. 68–202.

ÍF 29. *Fagrskinna*, ed. Bjarni Einarsson, 1985.

M	Morkinskinna. See Andersson and Gade; I cite to their chapter numbers for M, not to those in Finnur Jónsson's *Morkinskinna*, Samfund til udgivelse af gammel nordisk literature 53 (Copenhagen, 1932).
McGrew and Thomas	Julia H. McGrew and R. George Thomas, trans., *Sturlunga saga*, 2 vols (New York, 1970, 1974).
NGL	*Norges gamle Love indtil 1387*, vol. 1, ed. R. Keyser and P.A. Munch (Christiania [Oslo], 1846).
Sturlunga saga	*Sturlunga saga*, eds. Jón Jóhannesson, Magnús Finnbogason, and Kristján Eldjárn, 2 vols (Reykjavík, 1946).

INTRODUCTION

Audun's Story is the tale of a resourceful and lucky man who spends all he has for a polar bear. I know of few short stories as good. And the tale would be widely acknowledged as being among the classics of the form had it not had the misfortune to be medieval, Icelandic, and anonymous, a star-crossed combination that gives everyone, except a handful of medievalists, 300,000 or so living Icelanders, and some well-read Scandinavians, an excuse for not having heard of it.

I am indulging the hope that this essay will interest more than scholars of Old Icelandic law and literature and the few medievalists of other lands who maintain a passing interest in the Icelandic sagas. It is on the polar bear I pin my hopes. The ploy is not purely cheap: the plot of the tale actually depends on polar bears being scarce in the medieval Scandinavian world, though their scarcity there arises for rather different reasons than it does among us. And even if polar bears were not now objects of our solicitude, they would still have an allure. There is about them, in the tale's words about its bear, an "exceptional beauty," a fearful symmetry.

This is a rags-to-riches story; almost a tall tale, but it is a story of character above all. To see how finely the characters are drawn, how intelligently they behave, one must understand the range of expectations in their world regarding prudence and rashness, risk and reward, value and evaluation, and how these intersect with a value they understood as "sagaworthiness," a notion which means to capture behavior that is not only praiseworthy but also good in the telling. In this tale the sagaworthy does not take place in battle or in feud, its usual terrain, but at the intersection of the moral and the economic, two domains the extent of whose interconnectedness, or the location of the border between them, still occupies us intensely today, for they are much of the battleground of the political, and much of the focus of the legal.

I will supply the background assumptions—legal, moral, social, economic, cultural, psychological—that will give sense, good sense, to the action and the actors. The how's and what's will be clarified, and most of the why's too. By the end, whatever made Audun, an Icelander of no account, decide to buy a polar bear in Greenland, paying for it with everything he had, for no other reason than to travel halfway around the world to give it to the Danish king will not have lost its craziness, but you will appreciate not just his charm, which is apparent to any reader of the tale, but also his intelligence, and that too of the two kings he must deal with.

A few words on the saga style for those new to it: terseness and understatement are prized above all; and with it comes an insistent irony and subtlety. It is surprising to a reader new to this literature how light and decorous the touch of the 13th-century saga writers of Ultima Thule was. Very few words get very much done; the anonymous authors, like Shakespeare or more than a few books of the Hebrew Bible, can give a character a lot of substance in a few lines. A medieval Icelandic narrative will not pretend to give inner thoughts, at least directly. What you will see and hear is what the characters in the story see and hear, and unlike Shakespeare they are given no soliloquies. In other words, you will have to discern motive the way you still do today, by watching what people say and do and then imputing reason or unreason, whim or calculation, passion or habit, to explain their actions.

The Icelanders, by the 15th century if not sooner, had come to call these short tales "strands," (*þáttr*, sg., *þættir*, pl.).[1] They were mostly preserved within longer sagas of the Norwegian kings as interludes or digressions, but they sometimes appear independently. For instance, two versions of *Audun's Story* are included as episodes in a much longer saga of King Harald Hardradi (d. 1066), while the remaining version—the one I make the subject of this essay—is not. There are some fifty or so of these tales, more or less, depending on how one counts, and they share certain generic features, which I will not detain you to recite, except for one: they often are self-serving accounts of Icelanders abroad as they interact with Scandinavian, mostly Norwegian, kings and magnates.[2] The stories tend to have happy endings from the Icelandic point of view, though some can end with hard feelings not dissipated. Many of them are accounts of the vagaries of gift-gifting, the politics of giving to

---

[1] John Lindow, "Old Icelandic *þáttr*: Early Usage and Semantic History," *Scripta Islandica* 29 (1978), 3–44.

[2] See Joseph C. Harris's able treatment of the genre issues in "Genre and Narrative Structure in some *Íslendinga Þættir*," *Scandinavian Studies* 44 (1972), 1–27; and "Theme and Genre in some *Íslendinga Þættir*," *Scandinavian Studies* 484 (1976), 1–28; on general matters of formal narrative techniques and on the *þáttr* theory of saga composition see Carol J. Clover, "Scene in Saga Composition," *Arkiv för Nordisk Filologi* 89 (1974), 57–83; and her "The Long Prose Form," *Arkiv för Nordisk Filologi* 101 (1986), 10–39, esp. pp. 30–39.

kings or receiving their favor and favors, and how much gift exchange is politics by other means. And none takes up these issues with more penetration than the story you are about to read, though in order to understand *Audun's Story* we will need to give close attention to some of these other tales as well, which will be presented in part.

This tale has much to interest legal and cultural historians, anthropologists, social theorists, economists, and even philosophers, as well as students of literature. The story's treatment of gift-exchange is worthy of Marcel Mauss—he having a passing knowledge of Norse matter—or of Pierre Bourdieu, and it is given less to mystification than Mauss sometimes is, and less to privileging self-interest as the foundational behavioral motive than Bourdieu consistently is. It takes on the excellent anthropological literature on gift-exchange and holds its own. It puts the lie to the view that members of a society cannot get enough purchase on their own world to see its failings, paradoxes, contradictions, and triumphs.

Some technical matters: dates, origin, versions

Audun's Story is generally thought to have been composed in the 1220s, though the earliest of the three manuscripts that preserve a version of it, Morkinskinna (M), was not written until some sixty years later.[3] The three versions of the story differ somewhat, at times in fairly pertinent matters, but they share identical narrative orderings and similar wording through such significant ranges that not many steps could separate them from a common written source.

I have a distinct preference for one of these versions; it is found in a late 14th-century manuscript, Flateyjarbók (F).[4] I have been teaching F's *Audun's Story* for years, for no other reason, initially at least, than that it

[3] Morkinskinna ("rotten parchment") is a chronicle of the Norwegian kings from 1030–1157. And though the ms M dates from the last quarter of the 13th century, it is quite certain that earlier versions of M existed and most scholars would place an original M in the 1220s; for a lucid discussion of M's textual complexities and of the various theories regarding its composition see Andersson and Gade, pp. 5–24, 66–72. The date of the original *Audun's Story* depends only to some extent on when the earlier versions of M were composed, for it is not certain that *Audun's Story* was part of the M author's initial conception of his *Haralds saga* or was a later interpolation.

[4] F is a magnificent codex of 225 folia. Identified also as GKS 1005 fol, F can be viewed leaf by leaf on the website of the Stofnun Árna Magússonar: http://www.am.hi.is/WebView/?fl=20; see further below n10.

appeared in the accessible and affordable Penguin classics where it also had the fortune to be blessed by Hermann Pálsson's talent for translation.[5] My preferring F now, however, is not because it fits like an old shoe, but because it makes better sense and is smarter than the other versions on issues that figure at the intellectual core of the story.

Pálsson bucked the fashion by translating F, but he did not succeed in changing the fashion. Virtually all accessible printings of this story in the original Norse and all translations in English, previous and subsequent to Pálsson's, prefer M.[6] (The third version is found in a manuscript named Hulda [H], dating from the last quarter of the 14th century; H's version of *Audun's Story* is a somewhat prolix expansion of M, but it does in one instance clarify a matter left obscurer in M and F.)[7]

The general preference for M is due in part to a belief that an earlier manuscript must be closer to the original. The editors of *Audun's Story* in the standard ÍF edition of the sagas justify printing M because it is "generally terser and older and seems to be original." Why fewer words should mark a greater likelihood of originality is not told. F, as will be seen, is written in typical saga style, possessing all the qualities of saga terseness and reticence.[8]

---

[5] Hermann Pálsson, *Hrafnkel's Saga and other Stories* (Harmondsworth, 1971), pp. 121–128.

[6] For a bibliography of M printings of *Audun's Story* in Old Norse see ÍF 6:cvii–cviii. M is the version English and German speakers read in the first months of learning Old Norse, it being featured in the standard introductory ON grammars: Gordon, Sweet, and Heusler. For English translations of M, see Arnold R. Taylor, "Auðunn and the Bear," *Saga-Book of the Viking Society* 13 (1946–53), 81–87; Gwyn Jones, *Eirik the Red and other Icelandic Sagas* (Oxford, 1961), pp. 163–170; Anthony Maxwell, CSI 1:369–374; Andersson and Gade, pp. 211–215 (M ch. 36). I cite the sagas to chapter numbers as they appear in the relevant ÍF volume. I also provide page references where I deem these to be necessary as in the case of the *þættir* which are divided into chapters. Chapter divisions of the Icelandic texts are maintained in English translations, and because chapters tend to be quite short, seldom longer than three pages, references can be easily located. Since many of the saga texts I cite are available in translation in CSI, I will only supply bibliographical references to translations in the footnotes for those sagas, mostly in the *Sturlunga* compilation, that are not in CSI. For the Morkinskinna *þættir* I cite to the translations in Andersson and Gade, unless otherwise noted, or when I make small changes for the sake of translation consistency with other texts.

[7] See below pp. 39–40. On H's relation to M I thank Kari Gade whose views, via email, I produce here. There is no English translation of H's version of *Audun's Story*.

[8] F has only about 25 more words than M. The editors of the ÍF edition have, in fact, confused F with the wordier H version, consistently misidentifying readings from H they provide in the notes as coming from F; see ÍF 6:cviii and pp. 359–368. Most of F's added details occur in the beginning of the tale, setting the scene more fully; the significant variations and additions will be flagged later in the discussion.

There is no necessary reason, in any event, why the F version could not be closer to a supposed original than M. That would depend on how many links in the chain of copies preceded the surviving versions and how intrusive or careless the scribes doing the copying were. We know that whoever compiled or wrote the Morkinskinna sagas of the Norwegian kings tended to pare down the *þættir* (short stories) he inserted; there exist freestanding versions of some of the stories to allow the comparison. And well he should do some trimming, since he would wish to avoid repeating information he had given earlier in his account.[9] But if M is trimmed from a more circumstantial hypothetically original F, its trimmings were not of the sort that left material duplicated elsewhere in M on the cutting room floor. As I noted already, F's *Audun's Story*, stands free of *Haralds saga*, but it does not stand free by much. For F too contains a *Haralds saga* which is very closely linked to M's version of that saga, and only a folium separates its last word from *Audun's Story*. And if that were not close enough, consider too that though the greater part of F dates from *c.*1387, F's *Haralds saga* and *Audun's Story* are grouped together in a 23-leaf 15th-century insertion to F.[10] Though Harald at the end of *Audun's Story* sends Audun back to Iceland with good gifts never to meet again, in the codicological world they have never been able to part company. But whether F or M is closer to the original is unknowable and nothing in my arguments depends on the temporal ordering of the variant versions.

Translating Old Norse into readable English does not present major problems but it does present a few. The sagas are written with a limited vocabulary. There is not much elegant variation. One must vary, for example, Old Norse *fara*, meaning to go, with to sail, to voyage, to travel, or risk dismissal from most readers.[11] But I somewhat stiffly translate ON *heimilt* as "entitled to" better to capture the legalistic and obligational tone of the term in Thorir's discussions with Audun about

[9] See Andersson and Gade, p. 24.

[10] On this "younger portion of Flateyjarbók" (fols 188–210), see Andersson and Gade, p. 6 and Jonna Louis-Jensen, *Kongesagastudier*, Bibliotheca Arnamagnæana 32 (Copenhagen 1977), pp. 65–66, who assembles evidence that this later insertion, *Haralds saga* at least, is itself a copy of a late 14th-century ms and corresponds very closely to M. *Haralds saga* takes up the first 17 (fols 188–204) leaves of the insertion. The remaining six leaves contain seven *þættir* the first five of which involve King Harald, *Audun's Story* (fol. 206r–v) being the second in line; see also n4.

[11] But see Robert Cook, "On Translating Sagas," *Gripla* 13 (2002), 107–145, who argues for preserving the Norse style of sentence structure and restricted vocabulary.

providing him passage on his ship (Pálsson more colloquially renders it as "welcome to"). And I have consistently rendered as "treasure" ON *görsemi*, which perhaps should have been elegantly varied in the interests of more natural Modern English prose as prize, priceless or valuable object, or gem.[12] My persnicketiness in this instance makes for an occasional strangeness to the modern ear, but I think it better, for my purposes, not to lose the consistency of the evaluational terms applied to the bear and other gifts.

As I indicated, I direct this book to general students of the humanities and social sciences as well as to saga scholars. I thus render Norse names in an Anglicized style in the text and partly too in the footnotes, omitting accents indicating long vowels and rendering thorn (þ) and eth (ð), as th and d. And thus too a certain invitational tone and the referencing of what to saga scholars and other medievalists would be elementary. I ask these scholars to endure the tone, the th's and d's, in the interests of making these most wonderful sources more widely appreciated. It may be a fond hope that this essay will be read by any but experts, but then maybe, against long odds, it will borrow some of Audun's good fortune.

[12] *Görsemi* can thus be used as a term of endearment as when Hallgerd Longlegs in *Njáls saga*, ch. 44 (ÍF 12), calls a certain Sigmund "a treasure" for composing scandalous verses about Njal and his sons. Losing his head trying to please Hallgerd cost Sigmund his head.

THE STORY OF AUDUN FROM THE WESTFJORDS
(*AUDUN'S STORY*)

There was a man named Audun, from the Westfjords, and of little means. He boarded with and worked for a man named Thorstein who was his kinsman. One summer a ship from Norway put into Vadil.[1] The captain, Thorir, lodged with Thorstein because that was the best place to stay. Audun provided the captain with good advice and sold his wares for him to people whom he knew to have good credit. The captain offered to repay him for his assistance, and Audun chose to go abroad with him. Thorir said he was entitled to passage on his ship.

Audun told Thorstein his plans, saying that he would have nearly exactly enough—once he sold his sheep to provide for his mother's support—to have three marks of silver left over. Audun intended her to be maintained at Thorstein's for three years.

Thorstein said he was likely to have good luck.

Audun went abroad with Thorir toward the end of summer, and after they crossed the sea Thorir invited him to lodge with him in More[2] where he owned a farm, a fine place. Thorir asked Audun what plans he had, "but first I'll let you know what I'm going to do. I'm heading for Greenland and you are more than entitled to come with me." Audun said he would.

The next summer they voyaged to Greenland and put into Eiriksfjord. The wealthier passengers took lodging there, but the others sailed further on to the Western Settlement. That's what Audun did and he found a place to stay there.

A Greenlandic hunter named Eirik had caught a polar bear, exceptionally beautiful, with red cheeks. When Audun found out, he offered to buy the animal. The hunter told him it wasn't prudent for him to give everything he had for the bear: "I know that you've just exactly enough."

Audun said he didn't care and bought the animal giving everything he had for it.

---

[1] At Bardarstrand in the Westfjords of Iceland.
[2] A region on the west coast of Norway to the north of Hordaland.

He then returned to Norway with Thorir, who invited him to stay with him again. But Audun said he would take passage on a cargo ship south to Denmark to meet King Svein Ulfsson and give him the animal.

Thorir said that it was very risky traveling with such a treasure given the great war between King Harald and King Svein.[3]

Audun headed south to Hordaland.[4] King Harald happened to be there at a feast. The king was informed that a bear, a real treasure, had just arrived. He sent for its owner.

Audun went to meet the king and greeted him. The king accepted his greeting and said, "Have you a great treasure?"

Audun answered that he did have a treasure, a bear.

"Will you sell it to me for the same price you bought it for?"

He said he wouldn't.

The king said, "That wasn't a proper offer. Will you sell it for twice the price you bought it for? Then you'd make a profit, which is fitting since, as you say, you gave everything you had for it."

Audun said he wouldn't.

The king said, "Will you give it to me then?"

Audun said that he was not going to.

The king asked what he wanted to do with the bear.

Audun said, "I am planning to go south to Denmark to give it to King Svein."

King Harald said, "Can you be so stupid a man that you know nothing about the war going on between our countries? Or do you think that your luck is so much greater than anyone else's that you can travel with such a treasure where others who've done no harm can scarcely travel empty-handed?"

Audun said, "My journey is now in your control. Yes, I have often heard about the strife between you and King Svein, but maybe I won't be harmed."

The king said, "I think it makes sense to let you continue on your way. Maybe you'll be a lucky man. But I want your commitment to give me an account of your journey."

Audun promised to do so.

---

[3] On the identity of the kings, see p. 15.

[4] A region on the west coast of Norway in which Bergen is located.

He then headed south along the coast and east toward Oslo and then across to Denmark where what money he had was all gone. He was forced to beg food for both himself and his bear. One evening he met a man named Aki, a steward of King Svein's. Audun told Aki about his trip and asked him for some food for the animal, which was at the point of death. Aki said he would sell him food. Audun said he had nothing to give for it: "I really want to give the animal to King Svein."

The steward answered, "I want half-ownership of the animal; you can see it will die any minute if you remain the sole owner."

When Audun considered the straits he was in he had no choice but to sell him half the animal.

They now set off to meet the king, and many people accompanied them. The steward greeted the king and stood before his table, as did Audun.

The king asked Audun what country he was from.

"I am an Icelander," Audun answered, "just come from Norway and before that from Greenland. I had intended to present you this bear that I bought with everything I had. I met King Harald and he gave me permission to travel as I wished, even though he failed in his attempt to buy it from me. But then, sire, I came to this man Aki when all my money was gone, and I was on the verge of death and the animal too. And now the gift is ruined, because he wouldn't help us, neither me nor the animal, unless he could own half."

The king said, "Aki, is it as the man says?"

Aki said he was telling the whole truth, "and for this reason I wanted to give him half the animal."

The king said, "Was *this* how you thought to behave—given that I made a little man like you into a big man—to interfere with a person trying to present me a treasure for which he gave everything he had? King Harald thought it good to let him go in peace, and he is my enemy! It would be fitting I have you killed. Get out of this country right now and stay out of my sight forever. To you, Audun, I owe such gratitude as if you had given me the whole animal. You are welcome to stay with me for a long time."

Audun accepted. But one day he said, "Sire, I wish to leave."

The king was slow to answer but asked what he wanted to do.

He said he wanted to go south to Rome.

Said the king, "If your purpose weren't so good I would have been displeased. I will also provide you with money and find some pilgrims to go with you." And he pressed him to come visit him when he returned.

Audun went to Rome, but on the way back he took sick and wasted away. He was all out of money, thin and wretched, and had to beg along the way. He returned to Denmark during Easter, to the very place the king was then in residence. Audun didn't have the nerve to let himself be seen, so he stayed back in a wing of the church. He resolved to approach the king when he attended evening prayers.

But when Audun saw the king and his retainers in their fine clothes, he again couldn't muster the nerve to let himself be seen.

When the king went back to his hall to drink, Audun ate outside the church as was the practice of pilgrims before they gave up their staff and scrip. Audun resolved that when the king went to night prayers he would present himself to him. But as exceedingly difficult as he thought it earlier in the evening, he found it even harder now that the retainers were drunk. When the retinue went inside the king turned around and saw the man who did not have the courage to speak to him and said, "Let that man approach who wants to meet with me."

Audun came forward and fell at his feet. The king barely recognized him. The king then took him by the hand and bid him welcome and said, "you've changed." The retainers laughed at him. The king ordered them not to do so, "for he has seen to his soul better than you have."

A bath was soon prepared for him, and the king provided him with the clothes that he had worn during Lent. The king invited him to stay with him and serve as his cupbearer.

Audun said, "That is a fine offer, sire, but I'm going to return to Iceland."

The king said, "That's a rather bizarre choice."

Said Audun, "I couldn't endure knowing that while I was living a life of pleasure here, my mother would be treading a beggar's path in Iceland. The time I funded for her support is now up."

The king said, "You are certainly one lucky man. That is the only reason that would not offend me for your wanting to leave. Stay with me until the ships are ready."

Audun said he would gladly do that.

One day toward the end of spring the king went down to the docks with Audun. Men were busy preparing ships to sail to various lands in the Baltic and Saxony, and to Sweden and Norway. The king and Audun came to a particularly beautiful ship which was being equipped.

The king said, "How do you like this ship?"

"Very much," said Audun.

The king said, "I want to give you this ship to repay you for the bear."

Audun thanked the king for the gift.

When in time the ship was ready the king said, "You are set on leaving now, and I will in no way hinder you. I have heard though that much of Iceland is without harbors and that ships are greatly at risk. It just might happen that your ship will be wrecked and the cargo lost. Then there would be little to show that you have met King Svein and brought him the greatest of treasures. Take this bag full of silver. You will not be penniless if you hold on to this money. Yet it could happen that you lose this money too and then again there would be little to show that you have met King Svein and given him everything you had."

Then he drew from his arm a ring, the greatest of treasures, and gave it to Audun and said, "If the worst should happen and you not only lose the ship, but the silver too, you will not be penniless when you reach land if you hold on to the ring. It then can still be seen that you have met King Svein. But I think it reasonable that if you have a debt to repay to some distinguished man, give him the ring, because it suits a high-ranking person. And now farewell."

He soon set out, following the route through Ore Sound and then north along the coast of Norway and finally to a market town where King Harald was. Audun, this time, needed a lot of helpers. He soon went to meet the king and greeted him. The king responded warmly to the greeting and asked him to drink with him. Audun did so.

The king then asked, "Did you deliver the animal to King Svein?"

"Yes, sire," he said.

"How did he repay you?"

Audun said, "First, he accepted it."

The king said, "I would have repaid you the same way. Did he repay you more?"

"He gave me food and a great deal of silver to go to Rome."

"King Svein gives many people money even when they haven't given him a treasure. I would have given you money likewise. What more did he give you?"

"He invited me to join his retainers when I came back north from Rome, a beggar, and at death's door. And he gave me the clothes he himself had worn during Lent."

The king said, "I think it only right that he shouldn't have refused you food or his Lenten clothing. It's no great deal to do well by beggars; I would have done so too. Was there still more?"

"He invited me to be his cupbearer."

The king said, "That was a great honor, and I'd have done the same. Did he further repay you in any way?"

Audun answered, "He gave me a merchant ship completely fitted out and with a cargo that is the best to come to this country."

The king said, "That was grandly given. I would have repaid you the same. Did he then stop repaying you?"

Audun said, "He gave me a large purse, full of silver, and said to me that then I would not be penniless if my ship wrecked off Iceland."

The king said, "That was nobly done and I would *not* have done the same. I would have considered myself quit once I had given you the ship, whatever happened afterwards. Did he finally stop repaying at this point?"

Audun said, "He gave me this ring and said it could happen that I might lose all my property, but he told me that I would not be penniless if I had the ring. He asked that I not part with it unless I owed some high-ranking man so great a debt that I wished to give him the ring. And now I have found that man, because you had the opportunity, sire, to take my life from me and make my treasure your own, but you let me travel in peace when others could not do so. All the good luck I have comes from you."

The king said, "There are few like King Svein, though we haven't gotten along, but I will accept the ring. Stay with me; I will have your ship equipped and give you any provisions you want."

Audun accepted, and when he was ready to set sail the king said, "I will not give you great gifts. Take from me a sword and a cloak." These were both real treasures.

Audun went to Iceland that summer home to the Westfjords. He was the luckiest of men. From him a good line traces its ancestry, among whom can be counted Thorstein Gyduson and many other good men.

PART ONE

THE CLOSE COMMENTARY

THE COMMITMENT TO PLAUSIBILITY

If this story has the look of a tall tale, its author has undertaken considerable care to shorten it, to make it believable. He situates his story in the real world of the eleventh century.[1] The kings Audun meets are real kings, who really were at war. King Harald Hardradi, whose life could provide matter for more than a few action-adventure films, ruled Norway jointly with his nephew Magnus from 1046 and solely when Magnus died in 1047 until his death invading England in 1066, less than three weeks before William's more successful venture at Hastings.

King Svein Ulfsson of Denmark ruled from 1047 to 1074. And if we cannot know whether Audun ever existed, a real person, Thorstein Gyduson,[2] d. 1190, mentioned in the last line of the story, whom we know from chronicles and other sources to have been a wealthy man, claimed Audun as his ancestor. Though the filiation is not specified, Audun could either have been his grandparent or great-grandparent. But the plausibility of the story is less a matter of real kings and real countries, than of real homely problems.

Audun has a mother who is dependent on him, and so real is she that he is obliged to fund her for three years before he can leave the country to get his story going. Audun would be subject to a penalty of lesser outlawry—three years exile and loss of property—were he to go abroad without providing support for his dependents for "six seasons," i.e., three winters and summers, since the Icelanders, following Germanic practice, often counted years by seasonal half-years (ON *misseri*;

---

[1] *Audun's Story*, for instance, plays with the rags-to-riches theme in a way that does not disown as wholly its association with that kind of fairy tale as does a homelier down-to-earth story of a poor Icelander making good abroad, also in M (*Asu-Thord's Story*, M ch. 68; ÍF 11:337–349). In that tale, Thord moves in with a rich Norwegian widow, Asa (whose name also soon comes to be attached to Thord's as a cognomen, Asa's-Thord). He manages her affairs well; they engage in joint ventures, mercantile and otherwise, and are commercially quite successful. Eventually he gets accepted by her well-born kin.

[2] His death by drowning merits mention in *Guðmundar saga Arasonar*, ch. 18, in *Byskupa sögur*, ed. Guðni Jónsson (Reykjavík, 1953), 2:167–389; also mentioned in *Konungsannáll* anno 1190, in *Annálar og Nafnaskrá*, ed. Guðni Jónsson (Reykjavík, 1953), pp. 1–74; and in *Sturlu saga*, ch. 16, in *Sturlunga saga*, 1:63–114; trans. McGrew and Thomas, 1:59–113, where Thorstein is also mentioned to have provided shelter for some outlaws.

OE *missere*). It is as if the laws had in mind the minimal amount of time needed for Audun to go to Norway, out to Greenland, back to Europe and then be able to get back home again to Iceland in time to refund his mother. The laws evince considerable concern about people abandoning their dependents: were Thorir, the Norwegian ship owner, to have given Audun passage with knowledge that Audun had not provided for his mother, Thorir too would have been subject to lesser outlawry, which in his case would have meant the loss of his ship and the portion of cargo he owned.[3]

But the insistent reach of Icelandic law appears even earlier, in the first paragraph of the story. The law required everyone to be officially attached to a household for a yearlong interval beginning every May before residence could be changed the following May. Should one wish to remain where one was, a new yearlong agreement had to be renegotiated. Audun's legal residence is his richer kinsman's farm, where he is in service. To be lodged at a farm not your own is to be *á vist* there. *Vist* presents the translator with modest problems, for it can indicate being a paying boarder or an honored guest, no less than being in service. The latter usage—service—is the usual meaning in the laws, mostly in the phrase *á* (or *í*) *vist*, as when Audun "boarded with and worked for" Thorstein; the former usage—boarder or guest—is variously rendered in the story as "lodged" and "place to stay." Thorir finds his *vist* at Thorstein's when in Iceland and Audun at Thorir's when he goes to Norway. But the word also has distinctly non-legal uses and later in the story it appears as "food" for the bear or "provisions" for Audun's voyage.[4]

We also know that Audun, though in service and described as of little means (*félítill*), is not without some property. He has sheep enough of his own to fund his mother and still have about three marks left

---

[3] *Grágás* Ib 15, II 124–125. The earliest Icelandic laws, known as *Grágás*, are preserved in two main codices which date to some time shortly after the middle of the 13th century. They are not official compilations and the status of the various individual laws in them is often disputed. Some may be obsolete, some are marked as innovations, and others may never have taken effect or were flouted with impunity. On the uncertain authority of these codices see Patricia Pires Boulhosa, *Icelanders and the Kings of Norway: Mediaeval Sagas and Legal Texts* (Leiden, 2005), pp. 43–58.

[4] The laws governing domicile are quite extensive; the legal domicile determined where a summons was to be issued and thus what neighbors were to be called to serve as jurors, and which venue—the proper local thing or the right Quarter Court at the Allthing—the case was to be heard; see, e.g., *Grágás* Ia 128–137, also II 269–279: see Miller, "Home and Homelessness in the Middle of Nowhere."

over, which means he had sufficient means to qualify as a juridical householder (*bóndi*) even though he did not own land or have his own house. The laws provided that if a man owned a debt-free cow or its equivalent for each person who was dependent upon him then he was qualified to serve on jury panels or on a panel of judges and was also obliged to attend the Thing or pay Thing-dues if he did not attend.[5] But absent coming into a farm of his own by inheritance or marriage, or by purchasing one with the resources he had the luck to have acquired abroad, Audun could expect to spend his entire life resident at someone else's farm, though with means enough to be a fully legal person, rather than being counted as a dependent.[6]

Then there is the bear. Surely this is folktale. How does one man cart a polar bear thousands of miles through the Northern world? Imagining this—and precisely because the story cares not to tell how it was managed—fills one's head with images of a cartoon polar bear, docile enough to be led around on a leash, as it equally bespeaks Audun's resourcefulness in managing the logistics of transport. Logistical problems arise only once in the story, at the crucial moment Audun arrives in Denmark, completely without means, and unable to feed either himself or the bear.[7] For the first time the thought of how much meat and animal fat is required to sustain a polar bear concerns us as it must have concerned Audun all along. The bear thus remains very much a bear. It is not a magical animal, except to the extent it turns out to be a marvelous repository of value.

Maybe the bear was a cub. The story could have said so, but given the travel times between purchase and presentation to King Svein, a cub in Greenland would no longer have been a cub in Denmark, though it may have been subjected to lessons on proper behavior in the interim if it had been one when purchased. The story's not making much of one man getting a polar bear from Greenland to Denmark might require us to suspend disbelief, but it may not have done so for a medieval Icelander. Other sources note on several occasions that polar bears were given as gifts by Icelanders to rulers in Europe. So when

[5] *Grágás* Ia 159, II 320. At least one price schedule dated to within a century of Audun's adventures provides that six fertile ewes, or eight barren ones, equal a cow; *Grágás* Ib 193.

[6] Contrast Audun's legal personhood with the condition of those classified as *ómagar* (dependents) for which see below at pp. 106–107.

[7] Polar bears need an average of two kilograms of fat per day to survive; see Ian Stirling, *Polar Bears* (Ann Arbor, MI, 1988), p. 146.

Isleif Gizurarson sailed to Europe in 1055 to be consecrated the first bishop of Iceland he brought with him a "white bear from Greenland and the animal was the greatest of treasures," using the same word—*görsemi*—that *Audun's Story* uses to describe its bear, and which Isleif gave to the emperor Henry III Conradsson. Gifts of polar bears are unusual enough to get noted, but nary a word about the logistics of transporting or provisioning them in any of the sources in which such a gift occurs. Bears, polar or otherwise, it should be noted, were not native to Iceland. When a white bear appeared, it was because it was shipped over from Greenland, or because it arrived on drift ice, which was notable enough an event to make it into the sources on occasion.[8]

Even the suggestion of a bear on a leash finds its way into the laws. A fierce dog must be kept narrowly tethered on a yard-long leash, so one wonders if that applies to polar bears too: "If a man has a tame white bear, then he is to handle it *in the same way as a dog* and similarly pay for any damage it does...A bear has no immunity in respect of injuries done to it if it harms people." Given a polar bear's strength it is hard to imagine a tether strong enough to restrain it, but however tame and amenable it might be, it was to be treated as a dog for purposes of liability. A tame white bear was thus allowed, but no such grace was granted to darker bears. Lesser outlawry was the liability incurred by the ship's owner for bringing a brown bear, or wolf or fox, to Iceland; even the members of the crew were to be fined three marks each.[9]

There is also the practical matter of real commercial trade. Audun gets his start by helping the Norwegian shipmaster sell his goods, and the nature of this help is crucial to making the extraordinary success that Audun manages in the world of gift exchange plausible. I will expand on this point later, because it is central to the story's insisting that Audun's long-shot successes are not completely matters of luck. And note too that ships in the story are not magically ready to sail

---

[8] *Hungrvaka*, ch. 2 (ÍF 16), trans. Guðbrand Vigfússon and F. York Powell, *Origines Islandicae*, 2 vols (Oxford, 1905), 1:425–458; see *Landnámabók*, S 179 (ÍF 1:219), where white bears, a mother and two cubs, arrive on polar ice; trans. Hermann Pálsson and Paul Edwards, *The Book of Settlements* (Winnipeg, 1972), p. 84. Ingimund gives one of the bears to King Harald Finehair; before that, says the source, Norwegians had not seen white bears; also *Vatnsdæla saga*, chs 15–16 (ÍF 8). Einar Sokkason brought King Sigurd a bear from Greenland in 1123 (see ÍF 6:c); see Gert Kreutzer, "Von Isländern, Eisbären, und Königen: Anmerkungen zur Audun-Novelle," *Trajekt* 5 (1985), 100–108.

[9] *Grágás* Ib 187–189; cf. II 374.

without requiring workmen to equip and provision them, or to unload their cargo when they dock.

The timeline of the story defers to the realities of dangerous ocean crossings. When a Norwegian merchant sails out to Iceland he must summer there for reasons to be adduced soon, and when he goes out to Greenland he is likely to have to winter there too;[10] it is a year commitment. In short, this story plays itself out in a world that is their real world. This is a virtue of all saga literature when the events take place in Iceland, but even here when they mostly take place abroad. In Greenland, where one can afford to lodge is an issue; and when in Rome, or on the way back, there is the matter-of-factness about pilgrimages ending in serious disease being rather more likely than ending in miraculous healing.

And though Audun almost dies twice, indeed three times, two of these brushes with death are not by facing dragons, ogres, or knights as in a romantic quest or test tale, but by starvation and illness. If there are dragons they appear in the form of Harald, a real king, to whom we can credit the third time Audun almost dies, and in the form of Aki, who operates no more uncannily than trying to drive a hard business bargain.

And the beneficent supernatural? Some critics have turned this story into a Christian parable, and there are textual suggestions allowing for modest interpretative possibilities along pious lines. But there are no divine interventions, or none that cannot also pass for routine workings of man or nature. There are no miracles, no invasions of the supernatural, no gods, no saints; and if God is given his due by prayer and pilgrimage he is not (nor are his saints) mentioned by name or invoked once. He is represented in the story by a reasonably pious king, an Easter holiday, and certain hints that some parables of scripture may be being alluded to, but nothing untoward or "medieval" in the bad sense of the term. The story's world of polar bears, kings, courtiers, stewards, and pilgrims is very much of this world.

It is the specialist in Old Norse literature who knows the entire corpus of these short tales of Icelanders abroad who is likely to see this tale as fitting a formula and to be all a matter of genre and convention. The

[10] See the H version where it is explicit that Audun and Thorir wintered in Greenland. Ships that made it out and back in the same summer were said to have traveled *tvívegis* (two ways); see, e.g., *Bjarnar saga Hítdælakappa*, ch. 3 (ÍF 3).

formula, as I mentioned, treats of Icelanders coming off well in dealings with Norwegian kings after which they return home to the windswept lavafields of Iceland. The tales bespeak an Icelandic fantasy of Icelanders mattering, even though they lived in the middle of nowhere, gazing more to Europe than Europe ever gazed out at, or even thought of, Iceland. They reaffirm the preference for home to the temptations of the glitter of success abroad. But the formula in this instance still plays by the rules of commerce, the rules of gift exchange, the rules of etiquette, and by expectations that are not merely generated by literary form, but by the social and legal situations depicted.

I am sounding like the saga scholarship of old which cared about little in these rich character-driven and intelligently-motivated tales unless it bore on the all-consuming question of whether the events actually happened as recounted.[11] All we know is that the storyteller cared to make us accept the tale as plausible and that he managed to send scholars on wild goose chases to verify the truth of the tale shows how well he succeeded.

Yet there is still something inescapably uncanny about the tale. The story consciously maps itself on to a couple of standard folk themes, universal and long-lived: the motifs of rags to riches and of the bumpkin who turns out to be a cagey sophisticate. The uncanny hardly lies in such well-worn storylines. The polar bear quietly participating helps. But mostly the uncanny seems rather to emerge from the particular genius of this tale's author to invest such standard fare with interesting characters, behaving with superb intelligence. It is not that Audun makes out like a bandit that beggars belief, for in the end the story makes its very believability a big part of its uncanniness. And then there is the deftness that makes the ending no conventional happy ending, but one that reveals that the characters understood precisely the complexity of the action in which they had been engaged. The excellence of a perfectly told tale is itself uncanny.

Audun's success does not happen by magic or by authorial trick; he gets the assist of a little bit of luck, true, but that luck is something less than it seems. We may find it incredible that Audun can talk back to

[11] Whether *Audun's Story* really happened was until Fichtner's essay in 1979 pretty much the sum and substance of critical attention the story was treated to. Still in this vein is Kreutzer, "Von Isländern, Eisbären, und Königen"; see Edward G. Fichtner, "Gift Exchange and Initiation in the *Auðunar þáttr vestfirzka*," *Scandinavian Studies* 51 (1979), 249–272.

kings or refuse their requests in the way he does and still live, that he can manage, maybe even because of his readiness to say No to power, to achieve his ends. Audun, more than we do, knows who King Harald is and his reputation for hardness, cruelty, and sheer opportunism. The only miracle in the story is one that Audun recognizes: that given the character of Harald Hardradi, he did not kill Audun and confiscate his bear. Audun therefore is much indebted to him. And yet the author even makes sure to wrest Harald's kindness, if that is what it is, from the realm of implausibility by accounting for it in practical terms, keeping his Harald utterly consistent with the Harald he inherited from other sources. For all his ruthlessness and hard whimsy, Harald is only once portrayed as a stupid actor in these sources: when he invaded England. Indeed, Harald figures in the Icelandic imagination as the "most intelligent of the Scandinavian kings."[12]

---

[12] M ch. 32, *Fagrskinna*, ch. 56 (ÍF 29:261), *Heimskringla* (ÍF 28:119).

There were no towns or nucleated settlements in Iceland, so there were no regular markets. A market would form any time a merchant ship put in to any of the large number of fjords and inlets mostly in the north and west, but also in the east. Norwegian merchants (or Icelanders returning from abroad) brought in goods, the most frequently mentioned being grain already milled to flour, and timber, but also tar and linen. Timber of building quality was not available in Iceland, nor were there likely to be sufficient degree days for a grain crop to mature except for a few places in the south and west, and even there not reliably.

Imagine yourself an Icelander needing to purchase a couple hundred pounds of flour and some building timber. The news spreads that a ship has put in to Vadil, and you live some thirty miles away. How are you going to pay for the goods you purchase? Is there a conveniently agreed upon medium of exchange? Suppose you have silver. Would a Norwegian merchant sell all his goods in exchange for silver and sail back with an empty vessel? Or would he take your silver and buy other Icelandic products with it to fill up his ship? Or would he rather insist that you pay him in Icelandic goods and refuse your silver?

It is likely though that you or he need not worry much about exchanging silver, because it is unlikely you would have any. We do not often see silver in the sources being handed over in payment for Norwegian goods. Then what do we make of the three marks of silver Audun cleared from selling his sheep after he funded his mother's maintenance for three years? He may have wanted to travel light, but it is more likely that the marks of silver are ways of stating value; they are units of account, or measures of value, not real silver. When the story was written in the early 1200s, and most likely already by *c.*1050 when the story takes place, the normal means of payment was cloth, a homespun woolen cloth called *vaðmál*, or on occasion a higher grade of specially woven cloaks. The value of *vaðmál* was often expressed in silver ounces so that a legal ounce (of silver) was the equivalent of six ells, about three yards, of *vaðmál*, with silver being notional and woolen cloth actually providing the means of payment. Sometimes even notional silver was dispensed with and value was stated directly in units of ells of cloth.[1]

The Norwegian merchant, in short, would sail back with a load of woolen cloth, not even fish at this date, to which might be added more compact stores of value, perhaps falcons, if the ship was full of cloth and cloaks. The point is that if the Norwegian was to get paid for his flour and timber, the Icelandic buyer was unlikely to have enough cloth woven until later in the summer at best. The merchant would have to wait until you literally *made* your money to pay him and not infrequently the merchant had to stay the long winter to get his payment.[2]

Moreover, consider bargaining positions: you may not want to load your horses with your woolen money before you have determined the quality of the imported goods and agreed on a price for them with the merchant. If you have already sunk the costs of transporting your means of payment shipside it puts too much bargaining power in the hands of the Norwegian. Should he see how well your horses are laden he might find, as was the case with Audun when he purchased the bear, "that you've just exactly enough." The burden of packing up your money and driving six or seven horses thirty miles to the ship might make it wiser to ride down to the ship without any means of payment, inspect the goods, and start bargaining from there, making a contract for future delivery and future payment. You might even bring along some horses bearing no load at all, to take delivery now and promising to pay later. Notice how our easy-to-transport credit cards give the merchant bargaining leverage. Were we to have to return home and load a caravan of pack animals to transport our means of

[1] The mark was properly a measure of weight, and given that Audun's silver is notional so is the mark. Thus it is that eight legal ounces of cloth is a "mark" of "silver." Legally acceptable *vaðmál* was to be two ells wide; see *Grágás* II 288 and also n6 in the Dennis, Foote, Perkins translation vol. 2, p. 349. Icelandic money and units of account are a quagmire of complexity. For a reasonably accessible treatment in English, see Bruce E. Gelsinger, *Icelandic Enterprise: Commerce and Economy in the Middle Ages* (Columbia, SC, 1981). At this time there was no formal coinage available in Iceland though King Harald had begun minting in Norway during the period in which this story is set (see ÍF 5:261 for images of the coins struck). The fast diminishing silver content of these coins figures centrally in another Icelandic short story, *Halldor Snorrason's Story II* (ÍF 5:263–275), discussed in part below pp. 34–35; see Peter Spufford, *Money and its use in Medieval Europe* (Cambridge, 1988), pp. 83–85.

[2] E.g., *Ljósvetninga saga*, ch. 1 (ÍF 10); *Vápnfirðinga saga*, ch. 4 (ÍF 11).

payment back to the merchant we might find it much easier to resist our desires to buy.

Here is where Audun comes in. He provides Thorir the Norwegian with some help, and the help takes the form of finding creditworthy customers, people who could take away the goods now and be trusted to have enough wool and access to enough people to weave it in time so that Thorir could collect his payment and set sail before the weather turned bad in early autumn, as in his case, or next spring if he must. The Norse term I have translated as "good credit"—*góðr skuldarstaðr*—offers a more vivid image of what is at stake. It means literally "good debt placement." This suggests that Thorir in fact releases his goods first, sets a settlement date to get paid, and waits. This accords generally with saga evidence; sellers were necessarily more than just sellers of goods; they were also extenders of credit.[3] It was Audun's special skill that he knew who could be counted on to pay, to come up with the cloth for Thorir. It was risky for the merchant, but then it wasn't cost free to store flour over the summer in damp Iceland either.

A Norwegian merchant might be well advised to trust his selling decisions to a local, who knew, in the similar words of another source, "where the best debt placements (*skuldarstaðir*) were" and who could save the merchant the sometimes lethal error of extending credit to the wrong sort of people. In the source just quoted, the broker, a certain Forni, was also providing the merchant with lodging: "the Norwegian returned [to Forni's] and told him that he had sold some goods to Solmund. But Forni registered disapproval and said Solmund would pay a poor return for them." Solmund killed the Norwegian when he came to collect payment for his goods.[4]

The detail about Audun's precise service to Thorir, about finding good debt placement, is missing in the more popular Morkinskinna version and it is crucial to giving a deeper sense to the story. It reveals

---

[3] See William Ian Miller, *Bloodtaking and Peacemaking* (Chicago, 1990), pp. 81–82.

[4] *Ljósvetninga saga*, ch. 1. One Norwegian merchant, who was thought excessive in reminding people about the debts they owed him, was murdered in a plot hatched by two local chieftains who meant to plunder the unpopular merchant's goods; *Vápnfirðinga saga*, ch. 4. The violence was not unidirectional. Norwegian visitors to Iceland might resort to rather harsh debt-collection practices. A certain Snorri is killed by a Norwegian for not paying a debt Snorri's servant owed the merchant; *Gudmundar saga Arasonar*, ch. 19. And another Icelander gets his hand chopped off by Norwegian merchants though the specific reason is not given; *Guðmundar saga dyra*, ch. 26, in *Sturlunga saga*, 1:160–212; trans. McGrew and Thomas, 2:145–206.

that Audun has a talent, a knack for knowing whom to release goods to, to people who are, as we say, good for it. In Iceland his talent is employed in small ways by offering helpful brokerage advice to visiting merchants (this may well be the first time he has done so) and has had little chance to develop itself because, as noted, there were no fixed markets, and no certain places where ships could be counted on to appear. But abroad? There his talent, already in evidence in homely matters of flour, timber, and homespun, will be involved with different kinds of wares and different kinds of credit risks. As between two kings to present a bear to, did he not choose astutely?

At this point, right at the beginning, we have no reason to suspect that Audun's particular skill for successfully brokering sales shows anything but a good head for business, such as the intermittent nature of business back then and out there allowed for. But by the end of the story one wonders whether Audun's skill lies in making people more creditworthy than they would otherwise be, by some sort of alchemy of his character's effect on others. Something about Audun elicits handsome repayment, and Audun does not always leave it to the repayer to decide how to reward him. When Thorir offers to repay Audun for his useful service it is Audun who suggests how the payment is to be made, not in flour or timber, but in passage abroad on Thorir's ship, which Thorir confirms is fully justified. And Audun got rather more than one trip from Thorir. He was also Thorir's guest for the winter and was further rewarded with passage out to Greenland and back, which Thorir still feels somewhat obliged to provide him.[5]

As economically told as this story is, the tale still carries what appears to be extra baggage. It is replete with repetitions and redoublings; in fact it is a twice-told tale, for Audun twice recapitulates his story that the narrator has already told us: once to Svein, and then again to Harald when he returns from Denmark. The extra baggage we must account for now is a more practical matter. Why the first trip to Norway and then back out to Greenland? What narrative purpose is served by that?

[5] The term Thorir uses when offering his voyages to Audun—*heimilt*—suggests a right, an entitlement, that Audun has to the passage. See *Ljósvetninga saga*, ch. 7, for another case of an Icelander who brokers sales for two Norwegian merchants; like Audun he takes his repayment in the form of passage to Norway and lodging with the merchants once there. This suggests that if Thorir was being generous to Audun he was not being egregiously so, at least as concerns the first passage to Norway and lodging. Apparently the value of the brokering services was admitted by the Norwegians to be quite high and was thus well remunerated.

Why not sail directly to Greenland from Iceland, buy the bear and get on with the story?

The author is more than merely filling time to make his story last three years so as to give Audun a truthful and acceptable excuse when he declines Svein's offer to stay on in Denmark as his cupbearer. It also makes practical sense to sail back to Norway first before setting out westward again. Thorir's initial venture was to take goods out to Iceland, collect Icelandic woolen cloth for which the most sensible market was Norway, not Greenland, where Norwegian grain would be the more profitable thing to carry. This also comes close to proving that Audun's three marks of silver was three silver marks worth of cloth, for why would Audun waste his trip to Norway where silver was cheap relative to its value in silver-poor Iceland, but cloth was relatively dearer? We do not know that Audun paid exactly three marks of silver for the bear, only that he paid all that he had, which by this time might have been somewhat more than three marks of silver, in whatever form that value was actually embodied.

The prologue to the tale also gives us the first instances of three themes or motifs that will figure prominently in the story. One is Audun's luck: Thorstein, his kinsman, said he was likely to have good luck. Such predictions seldom fail to come true in saga writing, especially when forming part of the incipit of a tale, even if in this case Thorstein's prediction borrows from the form of a conventional wish of success to someone about to set out on a long trip. We know from the start that this is going to turn out well just as we know in a tragedy that it will not; it is the vagaries of how, the ups and downs, that will occupy us, not whether, though how well will still come as something of a surprise.

The second is embodied in a phrase that appears twice within a few lines. I have rendered it as "exactly enough," where it describes the amount of capital remaining to Audun after selling his sheep and the amount the bear will cost Audun when Eirik states his price term: "I know that you've just exactly enough." The Norse phrase is *á endum standask* and the image it suggests is of something coming right up to the edge with not a millimeter to spare. The phrase seems to describe rather more than Audun's squeaking by with just enough money to fund his mother and buy a bear; it also captures figuratively a major character trait: his not quite unintentional brinksmanship.

The third is the refrain-like repetition that he bought the bear with "everything he had." This phrase, appearing six times, permanently attaches itself to the bear, and becomes in a sense the proper name the nameless animal bears. The payment of "everything he had," not unlike "just exactly enough," is actually a kind of price term that defines a special reserve of value the bear carries that has nothing to do with its being rare. It rather bespeaks a special way that particular kinds of risk relate to value in their world that run counter to standard understandings of economic rationality in our world. We will take up this theme in much detail but suffice it for now that even Eirik, a polar bear hunter, a man hardly averse to risk in his own life, thinks it imprudent for Audun to buy the bear with "everything he had." Prudence requires spreading risk, diversifying one's portfolio. Even tough Eirik knows that: "The hunter told him it wasn't prudent for him to give everything he had for it."

Audun and his bear, bought with all he had, then sail with Thorir back to Norway. The other versions of the story are explicit that they winter in Greenland. There are now no more than some fifteen months remaining of the three-year outlay for his mother and the tale has only just begun.

DEALING WITH KING HARALD

Thorir asks Audun to stay on with him again, but Audun refuses. This is his first of many refusals of an offer, but Thorir, though of higher standing than Audun, is not of such standing that when he makes an offer it qualifies as an "offer you cannot refuse." Those are to come, and Audun will refuse them too. Audun announces to Thorir his intention to take the bear to Denmark in order to give it to King Svein; and Thorir, as did the hunter Eirik, remarks on the imprudence of Audun's purpose, reminding Audun of the riskiness of traveling through a war-zone with items of great value.[1] We do not know when Audun formed his intention to give the bear to Svein. It does not look like a spur of the moment decision when he announces it, but when and however he formed it, he will hold to his intention with a tenacity, a stubbornness, that is so consuming, that it seems to overpower the will of kings, and even cause the cosmos in some uncanny way to defer.

Within two sentences the risk of risks appears in person. As it makes its way down the Norwegian coast the ship bearing Audun puts in in Hordaland where King Harald Hardradi happens to be attending a feast. The polar bear is big news and the king is informed of its arrival. Audun is sent for. The king asks if he has a *görsemi*, a "treasure." Audun says he does have a treasure, a bear. Harald then makes Audun an offer to buy the animal: "Will you sell it to me for the same price you bought it for?"

We might wonder at Harald's opening move. He soon admits the offer is not fair, but it surely has a sniff of threat in it, given that he is not only a king with considerable bargaining power, but he is also Harald Hardradi, who gouged out the eyes of the Byzantine emperor, Michael V Kalafates, when he left his service in 1042. That tale may have been embellished but it was a tale that Harald himself had cared to have embellished and spread about. He may well have been ruthless and hard—Adam of Bremen calls him "odious to all on account of his

---

[1] Note that no one questions why Audun might want to give a bear to a king. That makes sense. It is the risk involved in giving it to this particular king that does not.

greed and cruelty"[2]—but he also made sure that he had a reputation for being so, mostly by treating Icelandic poets very well who preserved his story in memorable and flattering form. Such reputation for cruelty had a magical way of turning his mere expressions of desire into credibly threatening demands.[3]

Harald offers to buy the bear and names the price: "the price you bought it for." We might wonder what precisely the expectations in buy/sell transactions are in a world that makes the opening move one that denies the seller anything more than reimbursement, without interest, for his wholesale price. Is that the standard royal discount? Or is Harald's offer, like so many conventional opening offers, not to be taken seriously, except as an offer to bargain, so that even the lowly Audun can risk declining without losing his head? But while kings might often higgle-haggle, like so many flea market vendors, with each other or with the mightiest of their magnates, or with popes and archbishops, if they decide to haggle with someone who does not even look as if he qualifies as a merchant of any dignity one might suspect that he may not be so much playing by the rules of higgle-haggle, as playing *with* those rules. If the story had a musical soundtrack, the moment Audun said No the music would indicate that he had just entered the valley of the shadow of death.

After Audun's No, Harald makes his next move: "That wasn't a proper offer. Will you sell it for twice the price you bought it for? Then you'd make a profit and that's fitting since, as you say, you gave everything you had for it." Harald is operating on two levels here. On one, he is negotiating with Audun; on another, he is taking over the narrator's function by filling in parts of the story we were not privy to. From Harald we learn that Audun had told Harald more than that he had a bear when Harald asked him if he had a treasure with him. He also told him how he acquired it, and how much he paid for it: with "everything [I] had." Harald, as narrator, tells us that Audun has already been playing narrator to his own story, offstage. The author is economizing, having Harald let us know what got told to him without

---

[2] Adam of Bremen, *History of the Archbishops of Hamburg-Bremen*, 3:xvii, trans. Francis J. Tschan, with new introduction and bibliography by Timothy Reuter (New York, 2002).

[3] See M ch. 13, also Andersson and Gade, p. 428n9. On threats and their credibility see Thomas C. Schelling's classic *The Strategy of Conflict* (Cambridge, MA, 1960), pp. 21–80.

the author having to put the words into Audun's mouth first for us to hear.

Harald doesn't seem to take offense at Audun's refusal to accept the offer to buy for double the initial cost. Harald takes it rather as an invitation to ask for a gift. Though asking for a gift after twice having one's offers to buy rejected might strike us as strange, it is not unheard of in the saga world. A failed bargain in *Njáls saga* (ch. 47) follows a similar pattern. Gunnar: "Will you sell me some hay and food?" Otkel: "No." Gunnar: "Will you give me some then?" Otkel: "No." And after the request for a gift is also denied a member of Gunnar's party threatens to take the food and hay anyway and leave behind what it was deemed to be worth.[4] In *Audun's Story* such a forced transfer could be a very likely move, given the biography of the person seeking the transfer, and the music would become even more ominous. Instead, Harald has his curiosity piqued, tinged with bemused incredulity.

Harald might be trying first to get a bear on the cheap by offering to buy it. As the story will reveal, if he can buy it rather than receive it as a gift he can keep his costs down. Asking for a gift may be interpreted as one way of raising the offering price since in this world, and even in ours more than we like to admit, there is very little room for such a thing as a free gift, except as a thought experiment. Odin himself lays down the law: "a gift always seeks its return."[5] If we can trust Harald's words at the end of the story, had Audun given him the bear Harald would have rewarded him with a ship and cargo, something rather more valuable than double the price Audun paid for the bear. But moving from the diction of buying and selling to the diction of gift-giving cannot be dismissed as really nothing more than offering a higher price, where "real" reality is about price terms, and the rest is all gloss. The diction of gifts might involve mystification, might indeed at times shroud in euphemism certain presently unavowable motives, but it is not "mere" mystification. The game of gifts is a very different

---

[4] This kind of forced purchase is dealt with by the laws under the rubric of *rán*, or strong-armed taking. Such forced purchase has interesting implications for modern theories of property rights. Consider for instance eminent domain; see Guido Calabresi and A. Douglas Melamed, "Property Rules, Liability Rules, and Inalienability: One View of the Cathedral," *Harvard Law Review* 85 (1972), 1089–1128, at pp. 1124–1125; see my *Bloodtaking and Peacemaking*, ch. 3.

[5] *Hávamál*, st.145, in Hans Kuhn, ed., *Edda: die Lieder des Codex Regius*, 3rd ed. (Heidelberg, 1962), pp. 17–44, at p. 41.

game, with a different set of rules, than the game of a conventional purchase and sale.

Harald might, however, be observing a certain etiquette, the etiquette of politely extracting a gift. There is a suggestion that the proper way to ask for a gift is by first asking to buy. Asking to buy is perhaps a hint that a gift would be welcome. But that does not help us explain why, if that were the case, the potential giver does not say his No to the offer to purchase without some qualifying explanation, some softening of the refusal, unless that No is also a conventional way of inviting the potential recipient to ask for a gift. The potential giver might think it somehow safer to let the other ask directly for a gift, to make sure that he is willing to be bound by the obligations acceptance of a gift brings in its train. It may be that there is more risk in offering a gift to someone who does not clearly manifest a willingness to receive it, than in forcing someone who wants to receive a gift to ask for it.[6] Or, more simply, it is probably that a request to buy is only sometimes a hint for a gift, and even if it is a hint for a gift, some people are notoriously oblivious to hints directed their way. Surely No has to be able to mean No as a first-order matter. It is more that with so many of our No's, as well as so many of our Yes's, it is not always clear exactly what proposition is being rejected or accepted, or how intense a rejection or acceptance our No's and Yes's represent.

Harald's and Gunnar's responses of following up abrupt refusals of their offers to buy with a request for a gift of the desired object would appear to be as much a non-sequitur in their world as it is in ours unless there were some expectation that consistent refusals to sell might be hints to the would-be buyer to ask for a gift. But the delicacies and indirections are such that they can be easily misread. Audun's No's as well as the No's of the man who denied Gunnar were true refusals to deal at all, but that was not completely clear to either Gunnar or Harald before they asked for a gift; they had to wait for an explicit refusal before they thought the possibility of getting the goods as a gift were foreclosed by mere refusals to sell.

The Norse practice of extracting gifts was not often as direct as some customs commonly found in the ethnographic literature, or in the travel accounts of European encounters with various natives, in which asking

[6] On the dangers of giving an undesired gift see below the passage from *Egils saga* pp. 124–125.

for gifts outright or hinting so obviously that no one could claim to have missed the hint was the norm. Nonetheless we find an occasional Norseman behaving in just this way. Shows of admiration for an object such as an axe or a ship can be construed by their owners as requests for a gift.[7] I suspect that there lingers in the expression of interest or admiration for someone else's possession a near universal expression of a wish or a fond hope, which can be ignored or acted upon depending on the situation, that the admirer would love to have it be his. Thus the six-year-old down the street who kept noting to my wife that our then six-year-old no longer played with this particular toy, did he? Such delicacy. Here the strategic problem becomes how to refuse such requests. Hard enough to say No to a six-year-old, but what if it were Harald who was making such an obvious hint?[8]

One can imagine Harald looking slightly quizzical, mildly amused, at these No's. What in the world is this crazy Icelander up to? But when Audun tells Harald that he means give the bear to Harald's rival and enemy King Svein of Denmark, one would expect the axe to fall. What kind of recklessness, guts, or sheer social ineptitude lets Audun defy the king like this? Chutzpah (there is no English equivalent) like this demands an explanation. What can Audun possibly think he is doing? He forces us to move interpretation to the psychological plane. And not only the reader is so moved, but Harald is too.

He immediately offers two theories to explain Audun's behavior. Sheer stupidity and ignorance is the first: "Can you be so stupid a man that you know nothing about the war going on between our countries?" Audun undoes the grounds of this theory: "I have often heard about the strife between you and King Svein." The other theory proposes a different kind of stupidity, the stupidity of optimism, of believing the odds are irrationally in your favor, or that long odds are always shorter than they are: "do you think that your luck is so much greater

[7] *Egils saga*, ch. 36 (a ship); admiration of horses elicits a gift of them in M ch. 20; see further below p. 35 for the case of Halli and the axe; according to Raymond Firth, *Economics of the New Zealand Maori*, 2nd ed. (Wellington, NZ, 1959), pp. 411–412: "to admire something belonging to another person usually meant that it was immediately presented to the person who praised it." See David Graeber, *Toward an Anthropological Theory of Value: The False Coin of our own Desire* (New York, 2001), pp. 174–175, citing Firth.

[8] Harald is more than willing to ask outright for gifts without seeking to buy first; see *Brand the Generous's Story* below p. 83. But in that tale Harald is openly testing Brand's gift-giving ability, and Brand is not in Harald's presence when the demands are made. The gifts are requested via an intermediary.

than anyone else's that you can travel with such a treasure where others who've done no harm can scarcely travel empty-handed?" Audun answers this frankly. He does not understand his luck to be in the hands of God, Norns, or Fates. Luck is not mysteriously remote, uncanny, or unfathomable. Audun's luck is sitting right before him: it is Harald. "My journey is now in your *control*...but maybe I won't be harmed." Harald now knows that Audun is neither misinformed, or if an optimist, hardly a vapid one, and so he decides to let such audacity have its chance. As did Thorstein when Audun left Iceland, Harald suggests Audun might well be a lucky man, and sends him on his way, but not before he actually manages to extract a Yes from Audun, who agrees to Harald's demand that he return to tell his tale.

How could Audun risk talking to Harald the way he does and still let the tale maintain its commitment to plausibility? Audun knows Harald is ruthless, but he also knows that there are other aspects of the king's character that make it not outrageously foolish to talk to Harald this way. There was more to him than hardness. For one, he was solicitous of Icelanders: "Of all the Norwegian kings he was the best disposed toward Icelanders."[9] And he proved his affection. During a famine year in Iceland Harald sent four ships filled with flour and imposed a price ceiling on it of three marks of *vaðmál* per "ship-pound."[10] He also permitted any of the poor who could manage the costs of passage to move to Norway. We can, it seems, assume the laws of supply and demand gave way before Harald's reputation for ruthlessness, for it is doubtful starving people would give Harald credit for mere good intentions if the flour-bearing sailors could not resist the temptation of extracting monopoly prices once they landed in Iceland. Evidently Harald's prices held.

---

[9] M ch. 32, *Fagrskinna*, ch. 56 (ÍF 29:261), *Heimskringla* (ÍF 28:119).

[10] In M Harald "sends" the ships; in *Heimskringla* and *Fagrskinna* he "permits" them to sail. One would hardly imagine having to encourage merchants to set sail for Iceland bearing flour in famine times given the prices they could command, unless that is, the king had already engrossed Norwegian surpluses. Whether it is "send" or "permit" the important thing is that Harald is seeing to it that the Icelanders are given some relief. The sources do not agree on the price Harald set. M has three marks; but the other two versions of *Haralds saga* set the price lower, at 120 ells of *vaðmál* per ship-pound, which is 24 ells less than three marks at the usual six-ell-per-ounce standard. Gelsinger, *Icelandic Enterprise*, p. 34, puts an Icelandic ship-pound at 276 pounds; but ÍF 28:119n1 claims the Norwegian ship-pound to be about 150 kg; a standard measure of a cargo ship's carrying capacity is about 20 tons.

Why the soft spot for Icelanders? We are told why. He respected and admired their poets and he cultivated them. They composed verses that preserved the greater part of his biography. In some sense they invented him, made him larger than life, with his willing connivance to be sure, for they performed their works about him before him.[11] And they liked composing for his benefit, not because he rewarded them generously, because he often didn't, but because he was, in some respects, one of the guild. He was an able critic of verse, and to please him by versifying about him one had to be more than a mere flatterer: the verse had to pass muster as verse. To get Harald's approval for one's poetry was to know one had made it to the top of the profession. Harald is something of a versifier himself and he is no easier a critic of his own productions than he is of those of others. In *Haralds saga* he recites a stanza before the battle at Stamford Bridge and declares it to have been poorly crafted and so composes another.[12] It was not, of course, as if his love of Icelandic expertise in poetizing was disinterested. Cultivating poets was good politics; they did much to secure Harald his name and with his name his threat advantage.

It was more than the Icelandic knack for poetry that drew Harald to Icelanders. He could trust them for having their kin groups so far away, for their being more dependent on him in Norway than Norwegians of substance would be. Two of his most esteemed retainers were thus Icelanders: his marshal, Ulf Ospaksson, and his old campaign-companion, Halldor Snorrason, about whom a story is told that bears directly on Harald's behavior as a purchaser and contract debtor and so bears some telling: Harald arranges to buy back a ship he had given to Halldor, but shorts him a half mark of gold on the price. Halldor says nothing at the time, but when he is ready to sail to Iceland (on another ship) he arms some men and breaks in on the king while he is asleep with the queen and demands that Harald pay the amount still owing. Harald, never easy to deal with, says he will pay tomorrow, but Halldor, who doubts it is wise to wait for the morrow, sees that

[11] M ch. 32; *Fagrskinna*, ch. 56 (ÍF 29:261), *Heimskringla* (ÍF 28:119). There are slight variations in the wording of this particular account in these three versions of *Haralds saga; Heimskringla*, for instance, adds that the performances also took place before Harald's sons.

[12] All three principal versions of *Haralds saga* preserve the account; see M ch. 50. For other examples of Harald as literary critic see M chs 21, 40, 43–44, 47, and as a skald himself, M ch. 13; in F he is called a "good skald"; *Sarcastic-Halli's Story*, ch. 1 (ÍF 9:261–295), for which see below n15.

the queen has a gold ring on her arm of about the right weight and demands it. Harald, who will quibble over grams or grains of weight in the face of death, insists that scales be fetched to make sure Halldor gets no more than what is owed him. The queen quite rightly sees that Harald is not properly assessing the risk: "Give him the ring he's asking for. Don't you see that he is standing over you with murder in his heart?" Harald hands Halldor the ring; Halldor thanks them both and clears out in haste and sails away.[13]

His dealings with Halldor notwithstanding, Harald gets pleasure out of bantering, especially favoring the wit of those same Icelandic poets who burnished his reputation, even when it came at his own expense.[14] Says one story: "[Harald] was a good skald and regularly hurled insulting barbs at people when he felt like it. And he took it better than anyone when he was the subject of obscene wit, *when he was in a good mood that is*." The story in which that passage appears backs up the claim with some examples. One directly pertinent to more than a few of our themes, involving the Icelandic skald Halli, will suffice:

> It is told that on one day the king was walking down the street with his entourage. Halli was in the group. The king was carrying an axe, inlaid with gold, the shaft wound with silver and at the top end of it there was a large gemstone set into a silver band. It was a splendid piece of work. Halli stared at the axe. The king noticed right away and asked whether Halli liked the axe. He said he liked it very much.
>
> "Have you seen a better axe?"
>
> "I don't think so," said Halli.
>
> "Will you let yourself be fucked for the axe?" said the king.
>
> "No," said Halli, "but it is hardly surprising to me that you should want to sell it the way you bought it."[15]

The king so enjoys the response that he gives Halli the axe: "Take it and make good use of it—it was given (ON *gefin*) to me and so shall I give ("sell," ON *selja*) it to you."

---

[13] M ch. 30; *Halldor Snorrason's Story II* (ÍF 5:273–275).

[14] There are exceptions to his good humor in this regard; see, e.g., M ch. 19. It is not always wise to make fun of Harald's father whose cognomen "sow" was the source of insults directed Harald's way. Yet even that insult does not always offend him. With *Hreidar the Fool's Story* (M ch. 24, ÍF 10:245–260), compare *Stuf's Story* (M ch. 47, ÍF 5:279–290).

[15] *Sarcastic-Halli's Story*, chs 1, 10 (F version). The story exists in two versions, one in M ch. 43 and, as with *Audun's Story*, in a freestanding and quite different form in F, where it appears immediately after F's *Audun's Story*. M, for instance, does not contain the incident discussed in the text to which this note is appended.

In short, Harald was accustomed to and enjoyed "mouthy" Icelanders who gave as good as they got. Audun benefits greatly from Harald's appreciation of a good tale, and of an artful performance. Since Halli bests Harald in the repartee he gets the axe, and since Audun is strangely interesting and with no end of courage, he keeps his bear and obtains leave to travel. Still, Audun had the luck to catch Harald on a day "when he was in a good mood."[16]

This encounter between Halli and Harald is rich in other ways. Staring at an axe works to extract a gift though it is hardly the case that the staring works as obligatorily as it might among the Maori.[17] The staring does not lead to a simple handing over; rather it leads, very much as in Harald's dealings with Audun, to bargaining about the price. It is a standard move in scholarly work on gift exchange to show that gifts are often little more than self-interested transactions, falsely veneered with a pretense of sociable forms of generosity, but really little different from commercial transactions or obligatory exactions. Here it is the other way around: what is in fact a generous gift is veneered falsely with the harder diction and forms of a sale. Thus Harald and Halli negotiate the price of a gift that is "sold," Harald giving Halli the axe using the verb *selja*, when one would expect *gefa* (to give) or *fá* (to present). *Selja* means the same as English "sell" as in to sell for a price, but it still retained its more ancient sense of to hand over, to give. This is a gift wittily pretending to be more interested and less generous than it really is in order to maintain the sharp pitch that informs the entire exchange. It should also be noted, though I will return to the matter, that there are no hard lines between gift exchanges and marketlike buy/sell exchanges. Each requires negotiating, strategizing, and each can operate ironically or with purposeful creation of ambiguity by playing with and off the idiom of the other.[18]

---

[16] The victorious Harald is in a very good mood following a battle in which he routs Svein and takes captive the old, and nearly blind, Finn Arnason; he takes delight in humiliating Finn with offers of quarter which Finn, in frustrated fury, refuses. Harald spares him nonetheless, partly for showing spirit, partly because Finn will take no pleasure in being spared in any event; see M ch. 42, *Heimskringla: Haralds saga*, ch. 66 (ÍF 28:154–155). On Finn, see also p. 66.

[17] See above n7; see, e.g., *Þorgils saga ok Hafliða*, ch. 12, ed. Ursula Brown (London, 1952); trans. McGrew and Thomas, 2:25–70, where a request for a gift of a particularly handsome axe is made in verse by a tenant-poet to his landlord. The request is denied, but the poet is given a reduction on his rent in exchange for the verse.

[18] For the gray zones separating, or not quite separating, gifts from the a wider range of different kinds of exchanges that also can use the idiom of gift exchange,

Note too how Halli's insult maps onto Harald's offer to Audun to buy his bear "for the same price [he] bought it for." This time it is Harald who would rather, as the joke would have it, avoid making a profit, for the price is stated in terms of negative value. But the negative value of the insults, unlike the negative value of the buggering, gets transmuted because of the cleverness and gutsiness of the exchange. The wit works like the philosopher's stone, turning dross to gold. I will let the buggering joke stand on it own, since the matter has been thoroughly dealt with by other authors.[19] There does, however, seem to be a fairly durable timelessness to such jokes. They were standard fare in the repertoire of saga insult, the Middle Assyrian Laws of 1076 B.C. show them current then,[20] nor had they passed into desuetude in my high school, and still seem quite alive in more places than we care to know, perhaps because they are now offensive in more ways than they used to be. They do not figure, however, in *Audun's Story*.

see Algazi "Doing Things with Gifts," 15, in Algazi, et al., pp. 9–27, and below pp. 116–117.

[19] I must note, though, that Halli's joke depends on not drawing as fine a distinction as is commonly drawn in the academic literature between passive and active roles in male homosexual intercourse. Presumably Halli, against the received wisdom, is equating Harald's being buggered to get the axe and Harald buggering Halli to give it to him. As one saga notes of the roles: "neither had it so good but the one who stood in front had it worse; *Bjarnar saga Hítdælakappa*, ch. 17 (ÍF 3). For discussions of the lavishly cultivated Norse buggering insult, the *níð*, see, among others, Carol Clover, "Regardless of Sex: Men, Women, and Power in Early Northern Europe," *Speculum* 68 (1993), 363–388; Kari Ellen Gade, "Homosexuality and Rape of Males in Old Norse Law and Literature," *Scandinavian Studies* 58 (1986), 124–141; Preben Meulengracht Sørensen, *The Unmanly Man: Concepts of Sexual Defamation in Early Northern Society*, trans. Joan Turville-Petre (Odense, 1983).

[20] Martha T. Roth, ed. and trans., *Law Collections from Mesopotamia and Asia Minor*, MAL (A) §19, p. 159.

GIVING THE BEAR TO SVEIN: THE INTERESTS IN THE BEAR

If the confrontation with Harald is understood by both characters, as well as by the narrator, to be operating in a high-stakes comic mode, that is not the case once Audun shows up in Denmark. The stakes remain very high, but the mode shifts; it is no longer comic. He arrives out of funds and he and his bear are starving to death. For the first time, though it will not be the last, Audun is reduced to begging. Enter Aki, a steward of King Svein. To the bargaining episodes between Eirik and Audun, Audun and Harald, and the bargains brokered by Audun for Thorir the sea merchant, we now add another.

Contrast the different types of duress afforded by bargaining with Harald, who can simply take the bear if he chooses, with the kind of duress starvation places Audun in with Aki. We might even add Eirik the hunter to this discussion: did Eirik name his price to be everything Audun possessed because he saw that Audun's desire for the bear was so consuming that he could extract the highest possible price Audun could actually pay? We do not, however, usually think of our desires for a particular object as duress, unless they come from an addiction. Eirik cashes in within the rules. Harald refuses to take advantage after some light- and half-hearted attempts to play with the rules to test Audun's mettle, but once his mettle is proved, Harald waives his bargaining advantage, in fact cedes it entirely. Aki tries to cash in but breaks the rules, even if he must be informed rather rudely that he has broken them because of his obtuseness to the proper demands of the situation.

Aki is an object lesson in how not to play the game. Even if gifts and sales are not always clearly distinguishable from one another, there are still rules and forms to be observed and Aki doesn't observe them. His ineptitude, or his impatient greed,[1] prevented him from realizing his best strategy: he should have *given* Audun what he needed and left it unspoken that Audun would praise Aki's generosity to the king. Then

---

[1] His vice is not greed, but impatience, unless it was greed that made him impatient, for greed could have been satisfied within the contours of the gift game, but one needs patience to play it well.

the king would either reward Aki or, if he did not, then it would have been incumbent upon Audun to have repaid Aki handsomely from the proceeds of the king's gifts to him. What Aki will be punished for is not that he wanted to cash in, but that he tried to cash in using all the wrong forms. Aki is in the tale to underscore the importance of proper form. Form, in these exchanges, is often the greater part of substance because proper form offers some, though fakeable, indication that the person at least cares to appear to do the right thing. Though we will return to the issue of motives later, adherence to form is a way not only of acting as if one were properly motivated, but it is also a way of cultivating proper motives.

Off they head to the king, and they have drawn a crowd, as one would expect with a white bear in tow. Once at the king's we are treated to Audun's first onstage narration of his tale, a restatement of what we have already heard and seen. He is careful to tell the crucial facts, the ones, that is, that go to the bear's value. He informs Svein that he went to Greenland to buy the bear, that he bought it with everything he had, that he met King Harald and refused his offers to buy, that Harald gave him permission to continue, that Aki spoiled the gift by extorting a half share. Audun tells his story exactly right, presenting himself as wronged by Aki, as miserable, as perfectly intentioned. There is something of the artist in Audun, no less than there is in Harald.

Though some might think Audun a tattletale, he is properly appealing to the king in the king's role as judge (and thus too as a pricesetter).[2] In the other two versions of the story Aki and Audun agreed at the time of their transaction to have the king judge the value of their respective interests, so it was understood from the beginning that both Audun and Aki were to present a "case" to the king. In the H version, there is a stipulation that Aki pay Audun the difference between the cost he

[2] Pricesetting is a good part of what private law must concern itself with, as when damages must be determined for wrongs, or disputed interests in property must be evaluated. The king as judge thus often involves the king as pricesetter, though the two roles do not always perfectly coincide. Recall earlier Harald setting the price on flour shipped to Iceland; see above p. 33. This is pricesetting as a market control rather than as a legal remedial measure, but with a bit of imagination, one could see Harald's effort to prevent merchants from gouging Icelanders during famine time, as an ex ante prevention of wrongs, that his setting the price on flour may thus be seen as a pre-judged measure of damages that would have been assessed in an ex post legal proceeding. In either case, whether determining the price beforehand or afterwards, price determination is taken out of the hands of the principal parties and set by a third party; see Calabresi and Melamed, "Property Rules, Liability Rules," above p. 30n4.

incurred feeding Audun and the bear and half the value of the bear should that value exceed Aki's outlay as Svein assesses the value.[3] In M the terms of the bargain are less specific: "They therefore agreed on his selling half the animal to Aki with the understanding that the king would make a total evaluation." What we can see Audun doing when he pleads his case before the king is in fact fully in accord with his agreement with Aki; he is presenting, in a way that Aki did not foresee, information relevant to setting the price of their respective interests by letting the king know that the price determination should also make allowances for Aki's wrongs, for his having horned in on the gift. In categories we would employ now, what Audun is doing is moving what Aki thought was purely a contractual claim into the realm of tort. These categories, of course, were not available to Audun, but if we think of the governing category as price determination, then what came to be known as contract and tort are subsumed within the basic justice-job of price (damage) determination.

There is a comic moment in Aki's discomfiture:

> The king said, "Aki, is it as the man says?"
> Aki said he was telling the whole truth, "and for this reason I wanted to give him half the animal."

Even Aki, to his own mind, had cut Audun some slack. Audun had no bargaining power; he was in complete duress and hence at Aki's mercy. Still Aki let him keep half because Audun, who we now know also told Aki his whole story, impressed him enough so that he too felt that no matter what, the bear had to get to the king and that its value was partly in having Audun and Audun's story attached to it.[4]

---

[3] Thus H: "and they agreed that Audun should sell Aki half the animal with this condition: they should both go right away to meet the king and he should appraise both the value of the provisions that Aki gave Audun and that of the animal; Aki was to pay Audun that amount by which the value of half the animal exceeded [his outlay]." H shows Audun making sure Aki pays fully half the value of the bear as determined by the king. Even in duress Audun does not lose his head for business. That Aki would agree to such a stipulation may simply be further proof of his stupidity, but it also might show that he was as he says in F (though not in H) taking care not to extract as much as he could have from Audun: "for this reason I wanted to give him half the animal."

[4] See the preceding note for how little Aki managed to extract from Audun's duress in the H version, and to a lesser extent in M. The F version again improves on H (and slightly on M) by having Aki extract rather more than what in H could be seen as merely an interest-free loan for the fair value of the provisions secured by a half interest in the bear. F suggests that the price of whatever Audun received from Aki

One can understand Aki's behavior, even if it turned out to be unwise. The emoluments of high level functionaries in the early medieval world were the benefits of taking a cut on tribute meant for the king. Kings colluded in this, farming out regions and tribute collection to retainers, on condition that certain amounts of tribute made it to court, while the rest could be pocketed by the functionary, and the more he could extract from the wretches whom he squeezed, the more the official could pocket himself, so long as the king got his usual "rent."[5] Aki can let himself believe that the king will reward him for making sure the bear got to him, that he waived taking full advantage of Audun. What then is different about this gift that so enrages Svein, that Aki cannot take his routine cut? What makes the king think this to be a case of ingratitude on Aki's part for the favor the king has shown him, rather than business as usual? What justifies his banishment, and as Svein says, his death?

Certain gifts to the king, it seems, are special. Routine tribute is one thing, but a polar bear, a polar bear bought with everything the presenter had? And there is more than that. Examine the interests, as property law teachers would say, in the bear. By one view Audun owns it, subject to his conveyance of a half interest to Aki, which conveyance, however, turns out to be unenforceable. But there are two other interests in the bear still to be accounted for: Svein's and Harald's.

When Harald lets Audun and his bear have passage through Norway to continue their way to Svein, Harald's spirit—to employ the Maussian metaphors of what imbues a gift with its obligatory powers to be requited—attaches to the bear.[6] Harald has now signed on to the gift,

---

would be half the value of the bear. For Svein to have banished Aki perhaps it makes more sense that what Aki bargained for is a percentage up to fifty percent of Audun's eventual take. But none of the versions support that interpretation. The synoptic view the versions seem to point to understands there to be two methods of pricing the bear: one price, the one that Svein was to judge, governs the terms of the contract Audun and Aki negotiated. That price would exclude the value added by Audun's risk taking; it would be the price of a polar bear with no special story attached to it, which given the rarity of polar bears would still be quite high. The other price, the determination of which is the substance of the tale itself, is the bear's value as a gift with *Audun's Story* attached to it.

[5] There are more than a few cases in the sagas of royal agents being suspected of taking more than their proper share of the Lapp tribute destined at least in part for the Norwegian king; see *Egils saga*, chs 7–17; M chs 43, 48, 70.

[6] See Hans van Wees, "Reciprocity in Anthropological Theory," in *Reciprocity in Ancient Greece*, eds. Christopher Gill, Norman Postlethwaite, and Richard Seaford (Oxford, 1998), pp. 13–50, for a critical introduction to the anthropological gift-exchange literature. For

endorsed it. But he has done more than that: if Audun, by common understanding, gives Svein the bear, Harald, by the understanding of three key characters, has made a gift of *Audun and his bear* to Svein. Harald does not just do Audun a favor, but does Svein one too. He did what Aki should have done: aided Audun's mission or at a minimum not taken easy advantage of him when he was ripe for the plucking. Svein, when he blasts Aki, makes immediate reference to Harald's generous action, of which Audun took certain care to inform him:

> Was *this* how you thought to behave—given that I made a little man like you into a big man—to interfere with a person trying to present me a treasure for which he gave everything he had? King Harald thought it good to let him go in peace, and he is my enemy!

Now consider Svein's property in the bear. Once Audun announces his intention to travel to Denmark to give the bear to Svein, any interference with his mission is no longer merely an expropriation of Audun, but one of Svein too.[7] Harald has not been averse to unrelentingly plundering Svein's kingdom in the previous few years. Yet something about this bear headed for Svein prompts Harald to restrain himself. It does not quite let itself be considered booty.

Aki's wrong is not just a wrong to Audun, but to Harald, and thus too to Svein. A transformation has taken place. The bear is in a process of value accretion that is almost magical. It is not a matter of market forces and scarcity, for the bear's value keeps rising, even when it drops out of the story at the moment it is presented to Svein. It lingers on only in the revelation and determination of its value in the countergifts it elicits; it is its transformation into other repositories of value that is almost fairy-tale like, as a beast that becomes, if not quite a prince, then a princely sum. Much of the remainder of the story, in fact, is about fixing the bear's value.

---

a detailed and imaginative reinterpretation of that literature see Graeber's consistently engaging and provocative *Toward an Anthropological Theory of Value.* The notoriously difficult Marcel Mauss, *The Gift*, is the obvious starting point on the obligatoriness of the gift; its obscurity (presumably unintentional), has allowed it to be invoked as the "*fons et origo* of quite divergent theoretical positions"; Jonathan Parry, "*The Gift*, the Indian Gift, and the 'Indian Gift'," *Man* 21 (1986), 453–473, at p. 455.

[7] A law of King Æthelberht of Kent (6th century) explicitly provides the king with a legal claim against anyone who interferes with his men who have been summoned to him; *Æthelberht* c. 2, in F.L. Attenborough, ed. and trans., *The Laws of the Earliest English Kings*, (1922; rpt. New York, 1963), pp. 4–5.

Svein happily accepts the bear and invites Audun to stay, but after a short time Audun indecorously says he wants to leave. The king's hackles rise. One does not leave court by one's own decision; one must obtain leave to leave. But Audun, resourceful as ever, undoes the offense, or more accurately, keeps what is perceived as a proto-offense from crystallizing into a true offense, by coming up with the perfect excuse: a pilgrimage to Rome. Fast forward to the next refusal after Audun returns from Rome and is invited by Svein to become his cupbearer, a high-ranking court position. "That is a fine offer, sire, but I'm going to return to Iceland." This time Audun comes up with what Svein says is the *only* acceptable excuse: "I couldn't endure knowing that while I was living a life of pleasure here, my mother would be treading a beggar's path in Iceland. The time I funded for her support is now up." Says the king, "You are certainly one lucky man. That is the only reason that would not offend me for your wanting to leave."[1]

Audun, by the thinnest of margins, manages to evade a dismissal as devastating as the one that was Aki's lot. Audun seems both to wish to flatter kings, and to thumb his nose at them. The two may not be inconsistent desires, nor is it the case that the latter cannot be a good way of accomplishing the former. But Audun is not "some fellow/ Who, having been praised for bluntness, doth affect/ A saucy roughness, and constrains the garb/ Quite from his nature." He seems to be incapable of behaving otherwise than by stating his intentions and desires directly. He also seems to be aware that he courts risk by so doing. But that does not mean he can quite help acting in any other way. It is the trait of his, we mentioned earlier, suggested by the idiom—*á endum standask*—that appeared twice in the tale's opening which evoked the sense of pushing up against the edge, of coming to a halt right before plunging over the precipice.

---

[1] Classic travel episodes in the sagas have Icelanders frequently turning down high favor at court in Norway or Denmark in order to return to the spare amenities of home in Iceland. This becomes an unintentionally comic leitmotif in *Laxdaela saga*. It is the distinctive mark of the *Audun* author to examine the motif in more nuanced ways, by explicitly putting the excuses offered for not staying in issue.

But why should that excuse him before kings who can expect, because they are kings, that people will suppress what in other circumstances they might try to excuse by a plea of "I could not do otherwise, for that is just the way I am"? We are rightly suspicious of the truthfulness or sincerity of excuses that claim the offender is disposed, as a matter of indelible character, to offend the way he does. Weakness of the will, a well-worn topic in moral philosophy, comes in a variety of guises, most of which we suspect are imbued with a healthy dose of bad faith.

Audun buys some room for excuse by being young, poor, Icelandic, and perhaps a country bumpkin, but he does not save himself by playing the rube. He saves himself with a sure social sense of what can work as an acceptable, even noble, reason for his decisions. A bare minimum of social competence, however, as well as a modicum of an instinct for self-preservation should be enough to make anyone who wished to refuse a king's generous offer of hospitality provide the excuses and apologies for his refusal *first*, and not lead with the refusal—thereby making it an *abrupt* refusal. And the refusal still qualifies as inappropriately abrupt even though Audun softens it a bit with "That is a fine offer, sire, but…", a softening that seems so rote as almost to call more attention to the peremptoriness of the, "I'm going to return to Iceland" that follows it. Like Harald, so Audun too plays with the rules, pushes at them, rather than follows them in the interest of smooth and uneventful encounter. One suspects Harald is motivated by a desire to make others more than vaguely nervous in his presence beyond the normal anxiety one might feel before any king. With Audun the motive is more a delight in operating at the edge, testing whether he can save situations by skillful remedial action made necessary by his own violating rules of etiquette he could easily have followed. By virtue of tactlessness, he tests his capacity for poise and aplomb.

The story, however, keeps hinting at another view of Audun's character, though in the end it rejects it. Audun, I have been claiming, is no fool, not even a holy one, even though he seems strangely blessed. Yet Harald thinks, and Svein for moments wonders, whether or not he may be a little clueless, in the manner of a type whom I shall call the fearless nerd, if one will pardon the colloquialism. The fearless nerd is a person so oblivious to social signals, that he can appear courageous or utterly reckless, yet with no sense at all of his own derring-do mostly because, to repeat, he is without a clue. And though the holy fool can also be characterized as clueless by his being socially out of it, the style of the fearless nerd is different.

Take the case of a person whose dominant trait is fussy persnicketiness, such that everything he does is colored by it: I witnessed the following in a New York subway car some years ago: a black man presenting himself so as to announce to the world he was a "bad dude not to be messed with" was seated smoking a cigarette, against the rules, obviously. A trim slightly built man (I imagined him an accountant or an actuary), the kind who presents himself as one for whom devotion to rules and making sure they are followed is the center of his moral and psychological being, looked down at the smoker as he stood a few feet away and said, "I am sorry, but I am sure you are aware, aren't you, that there is no smoking in the subway?" The tone was crisply schoolmarmish, smugly priggish in its confident rectitude. We, the witnessing passengers all thought, to the extent dread had not extinguished our ability to think: he has waded up to his neck in the River Styx, and is without an inkling that he has.

The bad man looked up at him, quizzically, took another puff, and slowly exhaled. He then flicked the noticeably unfinished cigarette to the floor mashing it into flamelessness, as if he were crushing the body and soul of his reprimander beneath the sole of his shoe. And lordy be if that wasn't the end of it. He had not succeeded, to our eyes, in frightening the prig a bit, who was oblivious to the allegory being forced upon the cigarette. Nor did he seem to notice the collective shudders and sighs of relief and looks of disbelief from the rest of us. But I am sure the bad man did, and that probably sufficed for his recompense, that though the prig was untouched, he had succeeded in frightening us who substituted our manifest cowardice for the prig's utter, but distinctly unvirtuous, lack of it.

The fearless nerd did not feel himself courageous. He did not even discern the risk, except perhaps the risk of breathing secondhand smoke. He saw a rule being broken and when he sees a rule violated he must—his character demands it—issue a remonstrance. He was perhaps pleased that he had done his duty, but if he thought he had experienced a tale worth telling, the tale he would have told would have been very different from the one I am telling about him. It would have been a tale of the decay of public morals.

I am not raising the view of Audun as a holy fool or clueless nerd as a strawman. Audun is no fool, but the tale raises the issue of his character and motives and teases us or sets us to wondering, much as Audun set Harald and Svein, Thorir, and Eirik to wondering, if he is not a little bit, how to put this delicately, "obsessively ill-advised" in his actions. The tale teases us with the idea that Audun may only be the beneficiary of a lot of dumb luck. And it teases us too because it plays off the expectations of the folktale motifs it both participates in and transcends: the wily trickster and/or the country bumpkin making good.

The depth Audun acquires as a character is that he consistently reveals that he is neither a country bumpkin, nor a wily trickster. He is too deep for any facile characterizations, for what the narrator succeeds in doing with Audun and Harald too, and even with Svein though to a lesser extent, is to make these characters something more than stock characters. They have a complexity of intelligence and motive that distances them from their folktale exemplars much in the manner Shakespeare transforms the stock characters in his sources into humans more complex and of greater depth than I could ever claim myself or anyone else I know to be. Let us reserve the issue of motives until we have more facts on the table. The story is only at the halfway point, the exact halfway point.

EGGS IN ONE BASKET AND MARKET VALUE

It is hard to avoid associating the refrain of paying for the bear with "everything he had" with Matthew 13:44–46:

> Again, the kingdom of heaven is like unto treasure hid in a field; the which when a man hath found, he hideth, and for joy thereof goeth and selleth all that he hath, and buyeth that field.
>
> Again, the kingdom of heaven is like unto a merchant man, seeking goodly pearls: Who, when he had found one pearl of great price, went and sold all that he had, and bought it.

What do we do with "sold all he had" without overdoing it? Let the tale set the parameters of how far we can push the allusion.

Audun's Story is quite explicit about certain matters of prudence and riskiness. And it complexly links this discussion to prospects of return, but not in a way that agrees fully with our present ideas of economic rationality. The problem is diversification of risk vs. putting all your eggs in one basket, the latter strategy being something no less imprudent in Jesus' day except in the special figurative sense Jesus means to indicate, nor in Audun's day as we saw Eirik the hunter warn him—"The hunter told him it wasn't prudent for him to give everything he had for it." Audun does not heed Eirik's advice. He is a risk taker, and puts all his eggs in one basket.

The story gives a nuanced account of the relation of risk to value, one that maps only partly on to the way we would understand that relation now and ends up affirming the virtue, or at least the sagaworthiness, of competing visions of risk's relation to reward. As for us, so for them: the bear is valuable for the obvious reason that polar bears are rare in Norway and Denmark. The bears must come from Greenland, or from Iceland, recall, if one happens to arrive there on drift ice. They also get an extra boost in value beyond that conferred by mere scarcity, by bearing the markers of the marvelous and the exotic. That added source of value still holds among us; the bear is a luxury good.

But here is the big difference: the bear in Audun's world, unlike ours, takes on added value because its purchaser took an irrational risk when he bought it. Audun bought it with everything he had. That very fact becomes part of the bear's legacy, even part of its name. It no longer is a mere bear, but it is the bear-that-Audun-bought-with-everything-he-had. Svein thinks that adds value to it, as does Harald, and clearly, so does Audun who takes care never to forget to mention that particular detail in any account he gives about the bear, making it as I said earlier, something of a refrain in the story.

The risk of bringing a polar bear to Denmark from Greenland through a warzone, the risk of the bear dying, of the ship transporting it sinking or being smashed to pieces on rocks or reef, or of Harald or some brigand stealing it, are the kinds of risks that would figure in its value today, but not that the purveyor of the bear failed to lower *his* risks in acquiring it by not diversifying his assets. The market today could care less about that, except in one regard that cuts the other way: should a would-be purchaser of the bear discover that the current owner (Audun) had put all his eggs in one basket when he acquired the bear it would enhance the bargaining power of the would-be purchaser, in effect lowering the probabilities of Audun capturing as much of the value of the bear as he would were he not so vulnerable.

The world of honor put a value on certain kinds of risk-taking that bore no economic relation to the pricing of conventional investment risk, as when we rightly expect, quite rationally and predictably, that a low-grade bond will have to offer a higher rate of interest to its purchaser than a high-grade bond. Indeed the risk-taking of the sort that makes Audun think it to his advantage to broadcast that he bought the bear with everything he had must be seen to spit in the face of economic rationality, or it would not add any moral (and in the end real) value in their world.

Contrast Jesus' spitting in the face of the same economic rationality. His counsel cannot disguise the paradox, which is more effectively disguised in Audun's world: Jesus says the optimally *rational* strategy, the certain way to get the highest yield on your investment, is to bet on heaven with all you have, though it might appear superficially imprudent and irrational to others because it turns its back on the standard prudential wisdom in this fallen world of diversification, risk-spreading, and bet-hedging. No one is this confident in *Audun's Story* about the relation of increased risk to maximizing the payoff. In fact the story goes out of its way to show how much luck—namely in the person of Harald—and subsequent skillful management—as in Audun's resourcefulness in turning Svein against Aki—had to intervene to save Audun from losing everything he had.

Jesus is saying I am offering you a sure thing; you put all your eggs in my basket and I guarantee a stupendous return. There is no such guarantee of a happy outcome in the dangerous world of war, Vikings, ocean voyages, poverty, and disease. To the extent the story is invoking Jesus' parable, it is bringing it back down to earth. *Audun's Story* shows that the reason his strategy of non-diversification works is that others can be so impressed by how imprudent he is that they will bail him out, not out of charity, but because they are impressed by risk-taking if not quite for its own sake then for the sake of sagaworthiness, which means not just any kind of foolhardiness will work.

The value of the bear is intimately related to the value of its giver, to the risks he takes, to the pizzazz he displays, to his fearlessness, to his ability to come up with the exact right answer in the nick of time, and as will be teased out later, to his proper motives, as measured by their standards of propriety. Remember that in Audun's world the rule of prudent diversification holds no less true than it does for us, as Eirik the hunter indicates and everyone else does too when they note the exceptionalism of Audun's behavior.

But there also exists a parallel world, the one that sets the standard for greatness, the world of honor and danger, which is the world that generates stories that thrill. These stories take a very different form from cautionary tales, which invariably are stories that counsel the wisdom of prudence. Tales of prudence are the ones parents and teachers tell to children and are a significant part of what makes children find adults such bores. Best to keep those lectures very short; culture generates a host of proverbs that make the point more briefly though the grace gained by brevity is soon spent in repetitiveness. For diversification: don't put all your eggs in one basket; for avoiding the irrationality of sunk costs: don't cry over spilled milk or don't throw good money after bad. And so on.

If there is a parallel to Jesus' parable in *Audun's Story*, it is one with a host of attendant ironies.

ROME: SELF-IMPOVERISHMENT AND SELF-CONFIDENCE

The entire trip to Rome and Audun's troubles on the way back are narrated in two sentences. Not a word is spent in Rome except the word Rome itself: "Audun went to Rome, but on the way back he took sick and wasted away." Yet Rome lies at the dead center of the story, 73 lines in the actual manuscript before he heads to Rome, 76 after he comes back. The story is obviously structured with Rome in the middle and, with the introductory prologue condensed into one unit, folds on the line Rome provides making a mirror image thus:

[(Prologue IS, N, Grlnd) [N [Dk [**Rome**] Dk] N] (Epilogue IS)][1]

But does Rome have a substantive centrality to match its formal centrality? Some have thought so and try to make the tale into a Christian parable. The story surely enriches itself with hints and suggestions in that direction as we have already seen, but it remains ultimately agnostic and mostly practical about the relation, if any, between Audun's pious pilgrimage to Rome and his good fortune. Piety is simply part of the mix, offered up to complicate further our sense of the multiple motives that move Audun. His pious trip hints, too, that perhaps one of the reasons why he chose Svein as the most appropriate recipient of his polar bear was in part to pay deference to Svein's reputation for piety.

Surely there is absolutely nothing that justifies one commentator's view that the story "seems to be arguing that all moral acts are motivated by a kind of selfless love which is the human equivalence of God's love."[2] So much for the playful and profoundly subtle exploration of social action that mixes matters of self-interest, piety, propriety, duty, risk, sacrifice, courage, gamesmanship, politics, strategic skill, stub-

---

[1] This is a classic instance of "ring composition" fairly common in oral narrative; see, e.g., Stephen A. Nimis, "Ring Composition and Linearity in Homer," in *Signs of Orality: The Oral Tradition and Its Influence in the Greek and Roman World*, ed. E. Anne Mackay (Leiden, 1998), 65–78.

[2] Anthony J. Gilbert, "Social and National Identity in some Icelandic *þættir*," *Neophilologus* 75 (1991), 408–424, at p. 417; more nuanced, though still too reductive to my mind, is Elizabeth Ashman Rowe's remark re *Audun's Story* in "Cultural Paternity in the Flateyjarbók *Óláfs saga Tryggvasonar*," *Alvísmál* 8 (1998), 3–28, at p. 22: "*caritas* leads to profits, and spiritual grace bestows secular good luck."

bornness, filial duty, and a keen head for business. The tale suggests, though, certain complex linkages that connect piety and propriety with bet-hedging, base-covering, and return on investment. Rome demands an explanation, some aspects of which I will postpone to a more general discussion of the propriety of Audun's motives and of the politics of giving upward to kings and gods.

Christianity makes certain forms of self-impoverishment a rational strategy: "sell whatsoever thou hast, and give to the poor and thou shalt have treasure in heaven" (Mk. 10:21). Audun lives in a world in which some forms of self-impoverishment can work to one's advantage, not just in the way Jesus suggests. An excellent student paper I received a decade ago argued that one of Audun's chief skills is to be able to manipulate and take advantage of the various meanings of self-impoverishment, secular and Christian.[3] In the secular domain, he does so by putting all his eggs in one basket and so arrives in Denmark destitute and a beggar, as we have seen; in the more spiritual domain he exhausts his assets making his pilgrimage to Rome and, true to the story's commitment to doubling and doubling back, reaches Denmark a second time no less destitute arriving from the south than when he arrived first from the north. In each instance his self-impoverishment yields better outcomes than had he not been so reduced.

Self-impoverishment becomes, in Audun's hands, a form of capital. Here we see an instance of Pierre Bourdieu's symbolic capital's ready transferability into old-fashioned real capital, as Audun's self-impoverishment works to raise the price of the bear independent of its pure market value, by raising the moral value of Audun. Audun and the bear seem to do each other big favors. Each drives up the stock of the other.[4]

---

[3] Thanks to Charlotte Gibson, Michigan J.D., 1998, whose ideas I am modifying somewhat here. Paper on file with me.

[4] For Pierre Bourdieu symbolic capital and economic capital can each be transmuted into the other; see "Marginalia: Some Additional Notes on the Gift," in *The Logic of the Gift: Toward an Ethic of Generosity*, ed. Alan D. Schrift (New York, 1997), pp. 231–41, at pp. 234–235 and *Outline of a Theory of Practice*, trans. Richard Nice (Cambridge, 1977), pp. 177–178: "an accountancy of symbolic exchanges would itself lead to a distorted representation of the archaic economy if it were forgotten that, as the product of a principle of differentiation alien to the universe to which it is applied—the distinction between economic and symbolic capital—the only way in which such accountancy can apprehend the undifferentiatedness of economic and symbolic capital is in the form of their perfect interconvertibility." Bourdieu's opaque prose can prompt even French academics to complain; see Alain Caillé, *Don, intérêt et désintéressement: Bourdieu,*

Audun hardly could have planned to have gotten so ill on the way back from Rome that he came close, once again, to dying, though he would surely know that that was a risk he took. Other Icelandic sources suggest that getting sick on the way back from Rome was hardly surprising. The rich Icelandic woman Thorlaug was reported to have been seen on her way back from Rome, "poor and rather sick"; she died soon thereafter. Of Mani the poet it is said when he presented himself to King Magnus: "He had just come from Rome and had become a vagrant...Mani did not look good. He had his head shaven, and was thin and he had scarcely any clothing."[5] Mani does not put his impoverishment and illness to any use, but Audun even turns that, by some alchemical rendition, to his advantage.

Audun arrives more dead than alive on Easter, no less. He then undergoes a resurrection of sorts, as he is bathed—his spiritual purity obviously did not smell very good to anyone at court—and reclothed in royal raiment. No, he is not Christ, though the author means to suggest the success of his pilgrimage as doing exactly what it was meant to do: purify his soul at the expense of his body. That he is in a state of ritual purity is strongly suggested, and Svein draws out that lesson clearly when he reprimands the courtiers for laughing at his miserable appearance: "The king ordered them not to [laugh at him] 'for he has seen to his soul better than you have.'" One wonders if the sign of taking care of his soul was not so much undertaking the pilgrimage as almost dying doing so.

There lurks in this tale an ever-present questioning of the relation of self-interest to propriety, to proper motive, and the modes one employs to do well in the presence of kings and in the world in general. Has Audun, uncannily or maybe even consciously, astute as he is, undertaken

---

Mauss, Platon, et quelques autres (Paris, 2005), p. 73. Bourdieu also overstates the perfect interconvertibility of symbolic and economic capital; see the discussion at p. 131.

[5] *Sturlu saga*, ch. 30; also *Guðmundar saga dýra*, ch. 8; *Mani the Poet's Story*, whose tale is embedded in one manuscript (AM 327) of *Sverris saga*, ch. 85, in *Konunga sögur* vol. 2, ed. Guðni Jónsson (Reykjavík, 1957); trans J. Sephton, *The Saga of King Sverri of Norway* (London, 1899). The King Magnus of Mani's tale is Magnus Erlingsson, d. 1184, who died fighting Sverrir's force shortly after Mani visited. For other pilgrimages to Rome see *Thorarin Short-Cloak's Story* (M ch. 72). King Sigurd rewards Thorarin by giving him money to go to Rome and asks him to report back but the story ends with the remark that "history fails to relate whether they met again." The tale comes forty chapters after *Audun's Story* in M. In *Thorgrim Hallason's Story* (ÍF 9.297–303), King Magnus offers a half interest in a ship to Kolgrim who defers accepting, alleging a pilgrimage to Rome takes priority. His interest in the ship is held for him by his partner until he returns.

his pilgrimage to prime the royal pump? For surely what follows is an inundation of material wealth that he could not have predicted in his wildest fantasies. Was God answering his prayers, or was Svein playing the role of a pious king who undertakes to reward those God should reward by assuming the role of God's legate, God's purser? Nothing in the tale indicates that vulgar direct asking works to get you what you want from the person or deity asked: not even Harald gets his bear when he asks for it, nor does Svein get his requests to have Audun stay accepted. Indirection, or getting benefits as by-products of actions primarily undertaken because they are proper or grand or a nice thing to do in pursuit of other goals, seems to work best.

Some will insist on pushing the Christian theme, the resurrection of Audun at Easter, into more than the story can bear. Nothing in this tale will sustain a flat or mono-causal explanation of Audun's inner-states or of the source of his luck. The tale does not play by the same rules that govern conventional pious exempla or hagiographical writing, though it may for the purposes of its own complexity and ironic playfulness gesture toward pious themes.

It is significant, is it not, that the trip to Rome and back gets but two sentences, and that considerably more narrative resources—more than twelve sentences—in this very short story are devoted to Audun's sudden lack of confidence when he returns from Rome, to his social anxiety about his wretched appearance? This is the only time he manifests something other than fearless single-minded devotion to his stated undertakings and it is not piety that is motivating his sudden lack of nerve.

When Audun comes back he hides in the shadows of the church. He resolves to approach the king, but fails of his resolve, not once but twice (more of the story's narrative doublings). He has even fewer inner resources to announce himself to the king, now that the courtiers are drunk, when the king returns for night services.[6] This reticence runs so against the grain of Audun being a kind of "natural" in the Elizabethan sense, a Forrest Gump, a fool, a fearless nerd. Audun's ability to confront kings in confidence depends, we now see, on his feeling himself to be presentable, on being decently if not richly clothed so that he feels confident that he is presentable.

[6] See Taylor, "Auðunn and the Bear," p. 88, who notes Audun's uncharacteristic indecisiveness in this scene.

Audun, in other words, is not one of those people of mind-bogglingly undentable self-esteem who see themselves, no matter how wretched, boring, inept, or ugly they may truly be, as smart, talented, engaging, and attractive. True, like them, Audun's self-confidence depends on the vulgar cliché of "feeling good about himself," but, unlike them, he only feels good about himself when others are likely to concur with his self-assessment. Being ill and looking it, being dirty and reeking of it, and in the other versions of the story, actually having lost his hair, are the only things that ever undo his gift of self-possession. Even his necessary acquiescence in Aki's extortion, though it reduced him to a desperate lamentation, seems less to have confused him than to have mobilized his best rhetorical skills to destroy Aki before the king.

This shows that Audun does not behave the way he does from ignorance of the rules of self-presentation, whether before customers, sea-captains, kings, or courtiers. For him, as for most of us, acting well or charmingly means you have to present a good front, a respectable front. And though he could hardly have looked too good when he first met Svein, he was so hell-bent on his mission that that overcame any nice concerns about what he must have looked like. Besides, he was not then a courtier but a traveler with a gift to present the king that would more than adequately have excused any roughness in his appearance. But he has since then spent time in court, and he now holds himself to a more cultivated standard of presentability, even if these are but the rough standards of eleventh-century courtliness.[7]

His spiritual transformation (if any), to the extent it is partly owing to his sinking to death's door, so transformed his body that "the king barely recognized him." Trading his looks and health for a ticket to eternal glory was a price whose costs he feels excruciatingly. He understands and feels his appearance to be shameful. Audun is a person who is embarrassable. We had no idea for sure that he was embarrassable until now, there always being something vaguely "out of it" in his all-consuming mission to get the polar bear to King Svein. Who was Svein to him that he should ever form such a half-cocked idea? But Audun's manifest embarrassability for looking "saved" shows he still cares to play the game he set out to play in this world too, one of doing something sagaworthy. And so as part of his "resurrection"

[7] See C. Stephen Jaeger's attempt to push the origins of courtliness back to Ottonian times, especially among the courtier bishops; *The Origins of Courtliness: Civilizing Trends and the Formation of Courtly Ideals, 939–1210* (Philadelphia, 1985).

he is cleaned up, dressed presentably so that he can carry on, not as a new Audun who has thrown off the Pauline old man and put on a new man, but as the very one we knew before, one who has a truly magic touch with kings.

Do not misconstrue me. Audun did not go to Rome with bad motives, or because he was "operating"; we have Svein's word for that. Audun, though, is still playing in the games this world affords him, and he may not be quite able to suppress the knowledge, even if that knowledge did not provide his motive for undertaking the pilgrimage, that should he make it back, things might go very well for him indeed. We can dismiss once and for all that Audun was praying for a big haul should he get back from Rome. And though the pilgrimage and the terrible physical costs it imposed on him did not hurt him in the end, it hardly was part of a conscious strategy to milk piety for all it was worth.

There are other perfect touches in this scene. Consider the delicacy of Svein helping Audun overcome his reticence about approaching him. Audun is obliged to approach him, since Svein pressed him to come back when he set off for Rome. For Audun, this only adds more awkwardness to the situation because not to be recognized or thought to be a mere beggar when he was fulfilling his obligation to present himself before the king would be especially humiliating. Hence the king's perfect tact: "When the retinue went inside the king turned around and saw the man who did not have the courage to speak to him and said, 'Let that man approach who wants to meet with me.'" Svein even tries to have the retainers enter the church fi rst. Such tact shows that a certain dignifi ed civility was always a possibility, if not always the norm, as Harald's buggering jokes with Halli remind us.

A word on the laughter of the courtiers. Christianity has been trying valiantly for two millennia, with mixed success, to get people not to think human deformity and wretchedness to be a cause for mockery, ridicule, and laughter. Before that, the Hebrew Bible legislated against mocking the deaf and putting stumbling blocks before the blind (Lev. 19:14) and formally cursed those who purposely sent the latter down the wrong path (Dt. 27:18); one suspects, in fact one knows, that these strictures were not completely metaphorical. As early as 13th–12th century B.C. the Egyptian *Instructions of Amenemope* counsel not to "laugh at a blind man, nor tease a dwarf."[8] From the Olympians convulsed in

[8] See *Instructions of Amenemope*, c. 25, in Miriam Lichtheim, trans. and ed., *Ancient Egyptian Literature: The Middle Kingdom* (Berkeley, 1976), vol. 2, p. 160. What we might call the Thersites handicap, by which one loses his claim in court by arguments *ad*

merriment at Hephaestus' lameness in the *Iliad* to present reality TV to the classic sick jokes we (I) thrived on as an adolescent, the practice seems well-nigh ineradicable. Political Correctness, perhaps, more than even Christianity, which still countenanced, in some periods among some writers, taking delight in the suffering of the damned in Hell, has been quite successful at making much humor unsafe, at least in the academy, where wit of any source has never had a very flourishing life anyway.

But teenage sick jokes do not work in the manner of the laughter of the gods at cripples. The gods got no added charge from sinning against a norm not to laugh at the unfortunate, the wretched, the deformed, the ugly. That was how such unfortunate souls could expect to be treated; they were there to be mocked; it was all quite acceptable. Adolescent sick jokes, in contrast, depend on the thrill of violating a prohibition, one actually feels to be just. Svein's courtiers are only recently Christianized, and barely at that. If they feel any remorse for their laughter it would mostly be because it earned them royal displeasure, not because it jeopardized their souls or was thought uncivil.[9]

Clean him up and the old Audun is restored to an immediate manifestation of one of his most salient traits: saying No to kings.

---

hominem on the grounds of his ugliness or deformity, is known also in medieval lawsuits: "The opposing party charged him with lying and made fun of him, for he was short in stature, somewhat corpulent, and had what one might call a homely face. After many undeserved contumelies had been heaped upon him, he was unjustly condemned"; R.C. van Caenegem, *English Lawsuits from William I to Richard I* (London, 1990–1991), vol. 1, No. 204, p. 169, quoted and discussed in John Hudson, *The Formation of the English Common Law: Law and Society in England from the Norman Conquest to Magna Carta* (London, 1996), p. 54. At least Orderic Vitalis, the source of the report, considers the judgment made on such grounds a cause for blame. Homer's attitude regarding Thersites is more ambivalent, but the Thersites episode would not have been included if the merits of his claim did not unnerve some people. It was the undeniable forcefulness of the claim that motivated the toffs to riposte with arguments and beatings *ad hominem*.

[9] The motif of courtiers mocking a returning pilgrim is also found in *The Story of Thorstein from the East Fjords* (ÍF 9:327–332). These courtiers get a pious remonstrance from their king too. Though I note Svein's delicacy, court life in 11th- and 12th-century Scandinavia was hardly genteel, though the tasteful restraint and decorum of the saga style might give one a false impression in that regard. The mayhem that not infrequently attended retainers' drinking bouts led King Cnut to promulgate rules that required his men to leave field behavior outside the hall; see *Saxo Grammaticus* 10:18, in Eric Christiansen, ed. and trans., BAR International Series (Oxford, 1980), pp. 36–44; also *Konungs skuggsiá (The King's Mirror)*, ch. 37, ed. Ludvig Holm-Olsen (Oslo, 1983); see King Sverrir's sermon on the evils of drunkenness prompted by a drunken brawl among his men which resulted in significant casualties; *Sverris saga*, chs 103–104. Sverrir blamed German merchants for making wine too cheaply available; see further Bagge, *The Political Thought of "The King's Mirror."*

He declines Svein's offer to stay on as his cupbearer, alleging that the funding for his mother is exhausted and that he has no wish to turn her into the beggar he himself had only recently ceased being. The excuse this time is, as Svein says and as we discussed before, the *only* reason he could have offered for not accepting. This is rather more pointed than Svein's answer to Audun's first refusal of his offer to stay at court when Audun offered his intention to go to Rome as his excuse: "If your purpose weren't so good I would have been displeased." The possibility remained that there could have been other excuses that would have worked as well to extricate him from the offense he had just given for this first No to Svein. But this time the ante has been raised. One refusal of an honor, grudgingly pardonable; but two? And of an offer to serve as the first or second highest ranking person at court?

Although I tend to suspect any academic criticism that Lacanicizes or Freudianizes its subject as deeply wrongheaded, especially when it is imposed on medieval people, and tiresomely overdone even when not wrongheaded as when it involves people who have themselves been taught to understand their internal states in that way, I will risk noting—but make little of the observation—that Audun's first excuse to Svein invokes the Father or better yet the Papa, the Pope, since neither Father is actually mentioned; only Rome is. Audun is given no patronymic in his story either; and his descendant Thorstein Gyduson bears a matronymic; only Svein Ulfsson gets a patronymic.[10] Against this generalized unnamable Father, or a surrogate such as Svein, Audun, invokes as his second excuse (going home to Iceland) a very particular mother, *his* mother. This excuse, as Svein indicates, is the more forceful of the two, not that the obligation to his mother is not doing God's work, but as we saw at the outset, before it is doing God's work it is doing the work of the secular Icelandic law that requires him to support his dependents on pain of lesser outlawry.

[10] King Svein, it so happens, was better known in the English world by his matronymic, Estrithsson, for his mother was Cnut the Great's sister, Estrith (Ástríðr). His mother's blood gave Svein a modest claim to the English throne which he acted on by invading England, but gaining little more than some plunder and perhaps a bribe from William, he returned to Denmark; see the *Anglo-Saxon Chronicle* anno 1070 (E version). It may well be that Audun too bears his matronymic, which is frequent Icelandic practice when the father is otherwise unknown as in some cases of illegitimacy or when a father predeceases his young child's mother, as it seems Audun's father has, or when the mother comes from a more prestigious family.

One of the many brilliances of this story is that the mystical is given a human form, luck a human shape. God, unmentioned, is an obliquity, to whose institution on earth Audun pays deference, but Audun does not say he owes his fortune to Heaven, or to any sacrifices he made to its gatekeepers. How easy it would have been for the author to tag on such a piety. He makes you wonder what Rome had to do with Audun's good fortune, if anything at all, and keeps you wondering.

REPAYING THE BEAR

In the other versions of the story some time passes, enough for Audun's health to be restored, before Svein offers Audun the position of cup-bearer. In our version the request is made and denied right away. Then time passes until the weather improves in later spring and the ships are preparing for voyages. The king walks with Audun down to the docks to observe the bustle.

Now begins the payback. Svein asks if Audun admires an especially fine ship. Audun says he does. No doubt Svein's asking Audun's opinion of the ship is a fairly formal prologue to making a gift of it. Audun has to know what such a question is leading to, and hence knows exactly what form his answer must take regarding the attractiveness of the ship. No No's this time. Should he have felt it a middling ship he must express admiration, no less than we are obliged to praise the food the host puts on the table no matter how good or bad it may be. But in this case Audun's job is an easy one. He need fake nothing. The ship is a superb vessel and Audun accepts it with thanks.

The gift of the ship was fairly direct, a ritual of repayment clearly "for the bear." Now Svein shifts rhetorical gears. There are more gifts to follow, but these are justified differently; they are not said to be "for the bear." Svein narrates a hypothetical tale of future shipwreck and salvage:

> "You are set on leaving now, and I will in no way hinder you. I have heard though that much of Iceland is without harbors and that ships are greatly at risk. It just might happen that your ship will be wrecked and the cargo lost. Then there would be little to show that you have met King Svein and brought him the greatest of treasures. Take this bag full of silver. You will not be penniless if you hold on to this money. Yet it could happen that you lose this money too and then again there would be little to show that you have met King Svein and given him everything you had."
>
> Then he drew from his arm a ring, the greatest of treasures, and gave it to Audun and said, "If the worst should happen and you not only lose the ship, but the silver too, you will not be penniless when you reach land if you hold on to the ring. It then can still be seen that you have met King Svein."

That these gifts are a kind of insurance against shipwreck is so much pretense. They are meant to be marked by their supererogatoriness, their very excessiveness, because, as Svein openly admits, he wants to make sure concrete signs of his own reputation for magnanimity survive if Audun survives. Svein, under guise of concern for the dangers Audun faces along the harborless southern coast of Iceland, is concerned mostly that Audun continue to look good so that Svein can look good.

The arm-ring, though, is special; it is not like the other gifts. The ring is a conditional gift. Though Svein maintains the pretense that like the bag of silver it is insurance against shipwreck, in the next breath he cuts down on the title Audun is being given; in legal idiom, he "qualifies" Audun's title: "But I think it reasonable that if you have a debt to repay to some distinguished man, give him the ring, because it suits a high-ranking person." This ring is for you under certain limited circumstances, but should by chance you owe a debt to someone of high standing, it suits the arm of such a person. The message is discreetly given, again with Svein's usual delicacy, for he avoids any suggestion that it would not be appropriate for Audun, if Audun had no debt owing to a highborn person. The ring as insurance against shipwreck then is meant not for a wreck in Icelandic waters (for it is not supposed to be borne to Iceland), but in Norwegian ones.

Svein is in high performance mode. And he is playing to more than Audun and any courtiers present. He is, above all, playing to Harald. Svein has observed that Audun is a committed narrator of his own adventures, and he is now giving him the substance of the story he will tell Harald, pretty near dictating the lines. Audun is being asked, ever so subtly, to play the role we saw him play in the opening lines of the story: a middleman between the two real parties of interest to an exchange. And we suspect, as does Svein, that he will discharge it well, but who could anticipate how well? Again we see why the F version is richer and better motivated than the other two versions, which, recall, omit showing Audun acting as a middleman in matters of debt payment at the beginning of the story.

BACK TO HARALD: THE YIELDING OF ACCOUNTS

Audun fulfills his promise to Harald and returns, now a rich man, to tell his tale. Harald gets right down to business. He wants to know if Audun gave the bear to Svein and then, more importantly, how Svein repaid it. What follows is the giving of an *account* in the multiple senses of that word: a tale told, and a rendering of costs and gains.

There is an uncanny etymological recognition of a deep truth that links the idea of paying back amounts you owe (rendering an account) and the idea of having a story to tell. It is more than interesting that "to tell", as in "to tell a story", also meant "to count, to reckon", both in Old English and Old Norse, which meaning still survives in bank *teller*, who counts out our cash, or in the expression "all *told*", as when everything is counted up. In the Romance languages it is the same story. From French, English borrowed "count", "account", "recount". To account for yourself is to tell a justifying story, to tell a tale (tale, too, comes from *tell*), that shows you are quits with the world. Interesting too is that the relation of telling stories and rendering monetary accounts does not only occur in the Germanic and Romance languages but also in Semitic ones, so that the Hebrew root S-P-R generates words meaning count, number, story, book, author, and library. It is as if good narrative is necessarily linked to ideas of counting up and keeping track of gains and losses. In a nutshell, this is what drives tales of revenge, legal "counting", and exchanges in the marketplace or via gift. I must make amends for making my "fearless nerd" an accountant: accountants may be truer descendants of Homer than most contemporary poets are.

Harald wants Audun to tell his tale, to render his account, and that is what Audun will do. The scene combines both wry comedy with grandness of sentiment, setting up perfectly its powerful moment of recognition. It shows what a careful accountant Audun is. He leaves out nothing of value, no obligation unaccounted for or undischarged. Where we might start answering Harald's question—How did he repay you?—by enumerating the ship and cargo—the one payment Svein explicitly marked as payment for the bear—Audun starts by putting Svein's acceptance of the gift on the credit side of Audun's ledger, an issue we will return to in Part II.

The comedy, and Harald is well aware of the comedy since he is clearly playing it up, lies in his insistent questions, his dismissive observations at first—"I think it only right that he shouldn't have refused you food or his Lenten clothing. It's no great deal to do well by beggars; I would have done so too"—to his ever-growing amazement at Svein's generosity, which puts a halt to further dismissive observations. Harald takes care to match Svein, gift for gift.

> "How did he repay you?"
> Audun said, "First, he accepted it."
> The king said, "*I would have repaid you the same way*. Did he repay you more?"
> "He gave me food and a great deal of silver to go to Rome."
> "King Svein gives many people money even when they haven't given him a treasure. *I would have given you money likewise*. What more did he give you?"

And so on, as Harald assures Audun he would have matched Svein's invitation to join his retainers, his gift of his Lenten clothes, his offering him the position of cupbearer, and his gift of a merchant ship filled with excellent cargo. But that is as far, says Harald, as he would have gone. He concedes that Svein's adding yet a large purse of silver was more than he would have done.

The comedy depends on our doubts as to whether Harald would ever have paid as he says he would. We saw how Harald tried to buy the bear, though this, as noted, might only have been a way of priming the pump for extracting a gift. But the comic charm of the scene depends in part on Harald's willingness to pay, but to pay in funny money, to pay in commitments he will never have to put to the proof—I *would have* repaid you in the same way, I *would have* given you x, y, and z. Harald matches Svein's gifts with hypothetical "would-have" gifts. The only "repayment" we know he would have made is that he would have accepted the bear as a gift, since he asked for it as one.

Yet Svein outstrips in real gifts Harald's ability even to coin hypothetical commitments he does not have to pay. Svein's real generosity outmatches Harald's hypothetical generosity. Much is going on here. Harald knows he has a reputation for driving hard bargains and for being less than generous. One is therefore tempted to discount the amount he says he "would have" paid Audun, but he cares not to have his "would-haves" be dismissed as so much hot air; they are informed with their own kind of sincerity. And that is one reason Harald calls a halt at the bag of silver. That is more than he can entertain giving even as a thought experiment.

But then consider this. Harald would have been right not to reward Audun as greatly as Svein did. The bear is not as valuable when it arrived in Norway as it is when it arrives in Denmark. Svein has considerably more to pay for than Harald would have had to. In Norway the bear was a rare white bear which if it had been given to Harald would have merited the two-line mention Isleif Gizurarson got when he gave a polar bear to the Emperor Henry III. But in Denmark the bear has a substantially worthier biography than it did when it landed in Norway. In Denmark it is a bear that at the risk of death was denied to King Harald. The gift in Denmark has come to possess not only the value Audun's courage added to it, but also the value that it acquired, recall, by now also being a gift from Harald. It carries with it Harald's gesture of magnanimity, especially magnanimous because it comes from an enemy who chose not to dishonor his foe. There is comedy here too, for Harald's magnanimity takes the form of waiving a chance to grab something not his, whereas Svein's takes the form of giving away what already is his.

There thus might be good reason to take Harald at his word with his "would-haves" as stating what a reasonable and fair return for the bear would have been *in Norway*. Whether, however, Harald would have played fairly and given that amount for the bear is another matter. Halldor Snorrason, remember, had to collect from Harald by surprising him in bed and holding a sword to his neck.

Svein and Harald are engaging in a particular form of "fighting with gifts."[1] They are dealing with each other in the classic style described and theorized in reams of anthropological literature on competitive gift exchange, on the poison in the gift, and on the not-so-latent humiliation and one-upsmanship that is the dark side of convivial social bonding via gift exchange. Harald and Svein are engaging in a modified version of potlatch, a cultural practice more than any other that marked out anthropology as a discipline independent from sociology, and provided endless ammunition for intellectuals intent on finding ways to express dissatisfaction with capitalism.[2]

---

[1] Thus the title of Helen Codere's classic on potlatch appearing in 1950. Fichtner, in an otherwise learned piece, fails to notice the gifts that the kings are making to each other; "Gift Exchange and Initiation in the *Auðunar þáttr vestfirzka*." Though it is at the heart of the story, only Andersson and Gade, as far as I know, have noted "the contest in generosity" between the kings (p. 457n21).

[2] With Mauss, *The Gift*, ch. 4, cf. Graeber, *Toward an Anthropological Theory of Value*, chs 6–7.

Svein unleashes his generosity on Audun not only to reward Audun and to requite Harald, but to challenge Harald as to which of them is the more generous, the grander king. See if you can match this, Harald! Harald throws in the towel and concedes to his foe: "There are few like King Svein, though we haven't gotten along." But the gift of Audun and his bear from Harald to Svein is also an offer to test whether these two enemies can exchange more than raids, plunderings, killings, and engage in exchanges, still competitively mind you, that are more amicable or ultimately less costly than war. And this all converges to give the final recognition scene its spine-tingling perfection.

Harald has just admitted that he would not have matched the purse of silver:

> "I would have considered myself quit once I had given you the ship, whatever happened afterwards. Did he finally stop repaying at this point?"
> Audun said, "He gave me this ring and said it could happen that I might lose all my property, but he told me that I would not be penniless if I had the ring. He asked that I not part with it unless I owed some high-ranking man so great a debt that I wished to give him the ring. And now I have found that man, because you had the opportunity, sire, to take my life from me and make my treasure your own, but you let me travel in peace when others could not do so. All the good luck I have comes from you."

This is sublime.[3] Converging at this moment is the revelation of the astute understanding all three main actors had of the others' deeper designs. Audun understood Svein's instructions perfectly, because Audun is sharp enough to know that he owes Harald everything, and that Svein owes Harald something big too. We should never have doubted Audun to have a perfect sense of obligation and debt discharge; this was the precise talent that got him started in the first paragraph of the story.[4]

---

[3] Perhaps the biggest failing of the M version, and one which shows a lapse of judgment, if it were the case that the M writer pared down a longer original, is that it omits, "All the good luck I have comes from you." One might see in M's omission of this line (and also its lacking the detail about Audun's talent for finding creditworthy customers for the Norwegian merchant) as giving greater warrant for interpretations that wish to Christianize the story more than the F version can sustain. M leaves the source of Audun's good fortune less specified than F does. F wishes to make it more a matter of Audun's talents and, in Audun's view, of Harald's restraint. Did the M author engage in a small bit of pious excision, or did the F author add more explicit worldly practicality?

[4] Discounting for the short space in which this tale works its effects, its recognition scene bears some comparison with the unsurpassed conclusion of *Sir Gawain and the Green Knight*. Both treat of intersecting or nested games of exchange that are more

We also see that Svein understood Harald's gesture of good will in letting the bear through was precisely that, an advertent gesture of good will.[5] Why else does Harald demand Audun come back and tell his tale? Audun was an emissary from Harald. Audun knows that, and Svein saw that too. Consistent with the story's commitment to doubling and symmetry, Audun now plays Svein's emissary to Harald. And this time it is Harald's turn to display great delicacy: he does not thank Audun for the gift of the arm-ring, but praises Svein as he accepts, and asks Audun to stay. It is a perfect indication of his admiration for the game all three have played so skillfully.

Yet another word about risk: If Audun likes to add risk to his venture, the kings in this story seek to reduce the risks that attend the game they are playing. Audun is thus the perfect emissary between them because Audun is deniable. Harald can let him get on with his trip to Denmark, for if the signals of his conciliatory "panda diplomacy" are misread or rejected then the gesture can be denied as having been made. It was only a poor half-cracked Icelander of no standing and therefore his passage can mean absolutely nothing, or nothing that need engage Harald's honor one way or the other. If Harald directly made a gift of the bear to Svein, that would be too risky and might be read as an offer of peace or surrender rather than as merely an offer to play another kind of game to see where it might lead if it were to lead anywhere.

So too is Svein's gift to Harald deniable. That is partly the explanation for Svein's elaborate indirection when he gives the arm-ring to Audun claiming it mostly to be for insurance against loss of the ship. Should Harald decline the ring Audun tries to give him, the refusal can be dismissed as a refusal to accept from Audun, not a refusal to accept from Svein. Audun, in other words, provides a perfect way of eliminating

---

complex than the reader knows until it is revealed at the end. One key difference is that we are no less surprised than Gawain to find that such was the case for him, whereas in *Audun's Story* the revelation is not news to Audun, but to us: we find out that Audun knew all along that he was playing in two games, a starring role in one as the presenter of a bear, a supporting role in another as an emissary between the two leading men, the kings.

[5] Notice how Audun words hypothesizing what Harald might have done to him: "you had the opportunity, sire, to take my life from me and make my treasure your own." Audun does not imagine Harald taking the bear first and then killing him, or just taking the bear and sending Audun on his way, but in killing him first and then taking the bear. There is an implication that Audun would have fought to the death to prevent being dispossessed against his will.

most of the risk of humiliation for either of the kings should their overtures be rejected. And Audun gives the kings enough sense of his own competence and intelligence that they can trust that if anyone is good for this game, he is.

It should be noted that *Audun's Story* is inserted in Morkinskinna at a tricky moment in Harald's rule. Though he has been inflicting much more damage on Svein than Svein on him, Harald has also been engaged in purging magnates in Norway of suspect loyalty. A key one, a certain Finn Arnason, is mentioned as just having gone over to Svein in the last sentence before M's *Audun's Story* begins. This is a time Harald might wish to find some respite from the Danish war to consolidate his position at home.[6]

So who is using whom in this tale? Is it a story of a lucky and cagey Icelander who plays off two warring kings against each other to maximize an investment of all his property sunk into a polar bear? Or is it a tale of two very intelligent kings who take advantage of the opportunity provided them by an insignificant Icelander's crazy mission to send each other tentative peace-feelers?

I think the tale is clear on the matter: it is both. This is a true win/win series of transactions in the best expand-the-pie style. All three main actors gain, one and perhaps two gain economically, all reputationally, and two politically. Only Aki is ejected from the community of the story and even he would have been welcome to stay and would have continued to thrive had he made a gift of provender for the bear and food for Audun rather than selling it to them. Svein leaves with his reputation for generosity, with a dash of piety thrown in, burnished and monumentalized; Harald manifests charm, wit, with an ironist's genius at playing off his own reputation for cruelty and middling generosity. And Audun? He gets rich, and has one of the best stories ever told bearing his name. And as the story would have it, he is pretty much the author of his own tale, even if Svein must get a credit for scripting

---

[6] See M ch. 35. This chapter also tells of Harald's liquidation of Einar Thambarskelfir, who was renowned, when younger, for his skill as an archer, and of Einar's son, two of the most powerful men not pleased with Harald's rule. The episode is especially memorable because the immediate event leading to Einar's death centers on his reaction to a fart he emits while dozing off at one of Harald's feasts while Harald is evidently boring the company telling tales of his own adventures. The fart has elicited its share of scholarly comment: see Kari Ellen Gade, "Einarr þambarskelfir's Last Shot," *Scandinavian Studies* 67 (1995), 153–162, and William Sayers, "The Honor of Guðlaugr Snorrason and Einarr þambarskelfir: A Reply," *Scandinavian Studies* 67 (1995), 536–544.

the final scene. The prologue and the final lines are the narrator's, the rest can be seen as Audun's very own tale.

We might marvel that these Viking kings could be such masters of tact and discretion, but the dominant cultural, or at least the saga style that preserves the accounts, invites such lightness of touch because of its love affair with the irony of understatement. Understatement is the preferred way of making encounters pregnant with meaning, at once ambiguous, deniable, witty, and, not infrequently, threatening.

Lest I conclude this section on too upbeat a note I must add a discordant one: the positioning of the M version of *Audun's Story* would place it early in Harald's reign as sole ruler of Norway (*c.*1050). And the kings do not conclude their hostilities until 1064, two years before Harald's invasion of England.[7] It is thus wise that they took care to make their exchange of gifts deniable, as bearing any import beyond a minor diversion. Our F version though, by standing free from *Haralds saga*, lets us freeze in time a milder moment of mutual admiration between Harald and Svein, with nothing to dash the hope that that moment might lead to better things sooner rather than later.

[7] Finn Arnason's defection (M ch. 35) can be dated to *c.*1050. In 1064 Harald and Svein finally made peace (M ch. 42), the terms of which were that Harald got Norway, Svein Denmark and each was to keep whatever plunder he took during the long term of the war; see also *Heimskringla: Haralds saga*, ch. 74.

PART TWO

EXTENDED THEMES

AUDUN'S LUCK

Audun is a lucky man. He also has the look of a lucky man, for more than a few characters note it about him. His kinsman Thorstein "said he was likely to have good luck" right at the start. Harald, as we discussed, remarks on what he perceives to be Audun's own sense of his luckiness: "do you think that your luck is so much greater than anyone else's that you can travel with such a treasure where others who've done no harm can scarcely travel empty-handed?" And then, like Thorstein, Harald makes a prediction, hedged in the understated Norse style, but meant to have predictive force: "Maybe you'll be a lucky man." Soon people begin to declare him lucky without bothering to hedge. Thus Svein: "You are certainly one lucky man. That is the only reason that would not offend me for your wanting to leave." And finally the authoritative statement of the narrator in the final paragraph, when no dangers or doubts remain: "He was the luckiest of men."

Germanic ideas of fate, luck, and destiny have been much written about. I wish to narrow my focus to how this story plays with ideas of luck, for play with them it does. Start with some philology. The Old Norse words for luck that appear in this tale—in what is a blessing almost too good to be true for a story of gift exchange—are forms of the word *gift*. A lucky man or man of luck is a *gæfumaðr*, literally, a "gift-man"; luck is variously *gæfa, gifta, gipta* (gift), all reflexes of the root to give, *gefa*. *Gipta* is also, in a way to make Levi-Strauss salivate, the word for "to marry", the primal gift in his structural anthropology being one of a woman. That *gift* should also come to mean poison in German will give would-be wits the opportunity for a predictably bad joke about matrimony.

Take the name Audun, Auðun; the Norse form of English Edwin. The element "win" means friend. Put that aside, since it had already decayed to such an extent in Auðun as to have been unhearable as having once been *vinr*, friend, though the "win" in Anglo-Saxon Edwin would still be identifiable. It is the *Auð*, the *Ed* (*ead* in OE) that requires comment. *Auð* means riches and wealth; it also means luck or fate,[1] the

[1] Julius Pokorny, *Indogermanisches Etymologisches Wörterbuch* 4th ed. (Tübingen, 2002), I:76; Jan de Vries, *Altnordisches Etymologisches Wörterbuch* (Leiden, 1961), p. 18; as "wealth" *auð* is a masculine noun, as "fate," feminine.

linkage of the ideas being obvious. Luck and wealth go hand-in-hand. The verbal form of *auð*—*auðna*—meant to be fated, ordained by fate.

There is also another *auð* which means waste, void, devastation. Is that the dark side, the threat suspended by a thread over Audun's venture? As a pun, maybe, but not because there is any etymological connection between these two contrasting *auð*s. *Auð* meaning devastation does not share a root with *auð* as luck and wealth; the former only ends up a homophone with the latter by the accidents of certain sound changes occurring over the centuries.

Still, it is of interest that words that mean nearly the opposite of each other should end up homophones or bearing homophonic elements. Sometimes this is because they actually derive from the same root. The same Indo-European root, for instance, generates English black and French blanc (white) and English bleach or bleak, the original idea apparently referring to an intense burning brightness so that all color became indiscernible in whiteness, or indiscernible in the blackness of what had been burned to a crisp generating the brightness. And sometimes, as with the two contrasting *auð*s, one as luck and one as devastation, the result is a phonological happenstance similar to the one that had "to cleave" meaning to adhere and "to cleave" meaning to split fall together when their different vowels in Old English ceased to be distinguished in Middle English.[2]

We need not search for false etymologies and fortuitous homophones for the story of *auð* as wealth and *auð* as good fortune and luck; they are the same word. The etymological story gets better. The root that generates *auð* also generates *vað* as in *vaðmál*, the homespun woolen cloth, remember, that functions as money in medieval Iceland. The ancient Indo-European idea linking Auðun and *vaðmál* is weaving. What do the Fates do, whether as Norns, Moirae, or Parcae, but prepare wool, spin, weave, and cut yarn? Life and weaving become easy metaphorical extensions of the other. Weaving generates real wealth in the form of cloth and thus is associated with luck, and well-being; it generates images of growth and thus of life, and with life too come images of the inevitable wasting, wear, and tear, and final fateful cutting. Life begs to be metaphorized as a thread or a tapestry. And remember too that the Norse word for short story, *þáttr*, means strand or thread; what gets

---

[2] "To stick" derives from OE clífan, "to split" from OE cléofan. The uncanny way in which words often mean themselves and their opposites is the subject of a well-known essay by Freud, "The Antithetical Meaning of Primal Words," (1910), *Standard Edition*, 11:153–162.

woven are stories, or threads that are spun out, shaped, cut and given form, in cloth or in a life story, spinning a yarn.

This would be worth pursing in more detail but Fate is a weary topic, though I cannot resist a small point or two. The word for Fate in Old English, as most readers of this essay will know, is *Wyrd*, yielding Modern English weird, with the three weird sisters of *Macbeth* situated halfway between the Fates they are meant, in a twisted sense, to represent and being weird in our sense, unpleasantly strange. Wyrd/weird comes from a Germanic verbal root meaning "to become". But Wyrd too evokes the process of cloth production; its Germanic root goes back to an earlier Indo-European root meaning to turn, as on a spindle.[3] That same root provides the name of one of the Norse Norns, or Fates: Urð (who is Wyrd without the w for in Norse initial Germanic w was lost).[4]

This small detour shows that *Audun's Story* exists in embryo in his name: in short, Audun's name not only means destiny, it is his destiny. Luck generates riches, and it started out by Audun finding people who could weave and produce the cloth, *vaðmál*, necessary to pay Thorir, and then by selling his sheep that made the wool that produced the cloth to clear the three marks that were transformed into the bear. Weaving a tale indeed.

Fate as some grand oppressive cosmic force is not seriously present in *Audun's Story*, unless Rome's mysterious presence is meant to suggest it—and I do not believe that is what Rome means to do—but luck, as a more personal kind of gift, is. Nor is there any sense of fatalism, which we might define as a morbid view that eliminates the future tense, in effect turning it into a grimly ironical version of the past tense. That what will happen has in a sense already happened by irrevocable decree.[5] Not even the grandest, and in many ways the most pessimistic of the sagas—*Njáls saga*—has much truck with that kind of fatalism.[6] Though an occasional character will talk that way, none act that way,

[3] Pokorny, I:1156–157.

[4] See the still valuable Gerd Wolfgang Weber, *Wyrd: Studien zum Schicksalsbegriff der altenglischen und altnordischen Literature* (Bad Homburg, 1969).

[5] The Germanic languages did not have a future tense, but constructed it modally. Norse and English combined modals of intention and obligation—*shall* and *will*—with the infinitive to generate a substitute for a future tense, whereas German employs the idea of becoming or turning, using *werden*, the source of *wyrd*, *urð*, Fate, to do the same. These are rather different, almost opposite ways of understanding the idea of futurity, one emphasizing the will, one seeming to indicate its absence or pointlessness.

[6] On that saga's pessimism see Theodore M. Andersson, *The Growth of the Medieval Icelandic Sagas, 1180–1280* (Ithaca, NY, 2006), pp. 183–203.

for they continue to employ all their powers to act strategically and react intelligently to the troubles they face.

Luck operates differently from this kind of grand Fate. It is not even certain that luck can properly be seen as the small-time operations of Fate; it marches too much to its own drummer. Fate implies some kind of plan; luck implies nothing of the sort. It is more an inexplicable clumping of good things in some places and bad things in others, without reason if not quite without rhyme, the rhyme being the stuff of good stories, like the one we are dealing with. Fate can be inexorable, whereas luck seems too fleeting or too precarious for such a stern appellation. Fate suggests a determined order (though people often believe they can bribe or trick it, catch it nodding);[7] luck, on the other hand, though not dispensing completely with the idea of a Giver in its Norse conception, reserves to that Giver caprice and arbitrariness. Fate can deal with 1.0 probability and often does: death, for instance; it is rather the how and when of it that makes it worth trying to trick, or equally, the subject of tragedy. Luck deals with odds that tend to be remote, the kind it is unwise to bet on coming out the way you wish them to. Luck by definition means you beat the odds, whether it be good luck or bad. If we seem to think of Fate as more inescapable and certain, the luck of this story seems to be in good portion makeable by astute exploitation of the rare opportunities ambiguous and random circumstances present.[8] The presence of exploitable opportunities may be matters of pure chance, but the ability to be lucky enough to exploit the opportunities is more complex than pure happenstance.

Audun's luck thus manifests itself partly as talent or genius, in both genius's modern sense and in its ancient sense as a tutelary god or attendant spirit. Luck is a gift, just as *gipta* and *gæfa* would have it, but from whom? It seems it is partly conferred by something like a tutelary

[7] A belief in fate need not generate a psychology of fatalism. A belief in fate can in some systems coexist rather well with the belief that certain kinds of action can influence fate or trick it; see the nice discussion by Lisa Raphals, "Fate, Fortune, Chance and Luck in Chinese and Greek: A Comparative Semantic History," *Philosophy East & West* 53 (2003), 537–574, esp. pp. 537–538. Similarly, a belief in God's omnipotence does not preclude believing he may not be always omnicompetent; even a belief in his omniscience allows him an occasional blink or senior moment.

[8] Notice a general asymmetry in how we (and the Norse) often understand bad luck vs. good luck. The former we find it much easier to link with ideas of a primordial decree, with Fate, than the latter, which even if we believe in a beneficent God we often see as random, against the grain, dumb, pale in comparison to the greater power and likelihood of bad luck. Even amidst our plenty and desperate cultural commitment to optimism, we feel pessimism to be closer to Truth.

god, but that god does not appear to bear much of an existence independent of the character it informs; the tutelary spirit merges with the soul and flesh of the lucky man, so that Audun's luck is a talent that he is partly responsible for, to the extent that it is up to him to put it to use, to test it, and to train himself to capture the benefits and opportunities it might place in his way. Within limits to be sure, for Audun's luck is not only in him. As he well recognizes, it is also embodied at the most crucial moment in the person of Harald, who, bizarrely enough, for the duration of this story, is very much a tutelary spirit; his spirit not only informs the bear and so prompts Svein's behavior, but it also gives Audun a story to tell that is worth telling. Two versions of this tale (M and H), remember, saw fit to make *Audun's Story* a chapter in a lengthy *Haralds saga*.

If, as I just claimed, our luck is in part like a trait of character no less than are, for example, our sanguinity, irascibility, love of risk, generosity, intelligence, keen sense of propriety and right action or lack thereof, to what extent are we to be held accountable for our own luck? Luck seems to provide, in popular understanding, a reason for praise or blame. Whether this is justifiable in some grand moral sense troubles us at times, but it troubles us because of a deep urge to feel that there is something ineluctably praiseworthy or blameworthy about luck. Do you want to be friends with a person whose luck is consistently bad? Instances of bad luck, we feel, have a way of bringing more in their wake, and that unluckiness might be contagious too, a disease. We impose sanctions of avoidance and more serious kinds of legal liability on those who have bad luck. At some point, the accident-prone schlemiel, the loser, or sadsack (notice how many pejorative terms we have for such people) is someone who is seen as having it coming, as deserving his own misfortunes, and certainly deserving his very high insurance rates, or uninsurability.

And lucky persons? Once we view them as lucky, we want to participate in their charisma, for we feel that too may well be contagious. We reward the luck of one's genes by valuing the beautiful and naturally talented. And what do we call them? Gifted. The linking of the ideas of gift and luck with blessings of wealth and talent is still very much alive, much as the genius of Old Norse would have it, even though the word "gifted," in a transformation of values in the best Nietzschean manner, has come to mean a dull-normal student.

There is a strong sense in *Audun's Story* that Audun deserves his good luck, because he generates so much of it for himself as a consequence of his virtue, his intelligence and integrity, and manifest charm. One could argue, perhaps, that some cosmic principle, call it the God whom Audun pays homage to by undertaking his pilgrimage to Rome, is behind Audun's luck. Was it not this God's son who counseled putting all your eggs in one basket, imprudent as it appears, as the best investment strategy, advice that Audun heeds in worldly matters at least? But, as we discussed, the tale does not give much warrant for giving God the credit. We do not see God or any gods pulling Harald's strings, who, recall, is to whom Audun attributes *all* his good luck, not to God. And Harald does not make even the faintest nod to piety in the way Svein does. Harald's motives are irredeemably Harald's, and secular. He is tickled by this Icelander on a crazed mission; he sees the political possibilities of letting him get through to Svein and, consistent with the Harald of the stories told about him, he resists the urge to prevent a good tale from happening—especially one in which he plays a lead role.

One can readily see what makes medieval Icelandic literature so attractive: it is character and strategy all the way down. Allegory, tendentiousness, moralisms, though not completely absent in the sagas, tend to know their proper place, keeping modestly to the shadows where they seldom interfere with the efficient and intelligent representation of complex social and political action. There can be obligatory rote piety on occasion in a saga, but such intrusions are noteworthy for their rarity even when the saga action is set in post-conversion times. The sagas (the classical family sagas and *Sturlunga* saga as well) might test credulity with an occasional mound dweller, certain kinds of sorcery, some very corporeal revenants, prophetic dreams, or the ease at which a sword may slice through a body, but very infrequently by the intervention of God or his saints in human affairs.

A couple of issues remain on this theme that touch on our story. Given that Audun is suspected of being lucky right from the start, can he always count on his luck? We should qualify that: he is lucky once the story gets going, but his poverty at the story's start shows that he had not *yet* been very lucky. Do the lucky have inexhaustible supplies of luck or do they have to economize on their luck, and not draw on it too often? Audun almost dies twice of starvation and illness, and comes within a hair of getting killed by Harald. Better luck would have spared him these close calls and kept him safely above such testings of his luck, unless luck, real luck, must reveal itself by getting out of unlucky situations against long odds. Three times he is lucky, barely escaping close calls. Would you think he should risk a fourth, a fifth, or an nth testing of his luck?

Even a middlingly prudent person would answer No and Audun gave the same answer. His story ends with no further mention of sagaworthy behavior credited to his account. He is a presser of luck for three years and six pages. He is not about to engage in a lifetime of high-stakes risk taking. He won big once and the victory drew enormously on his supply of luck. *Egils saga* preserves a proverb to the effect. A father advises his son that one successful trip abroad is enough: "the more trips you take, the more various the outcomes."[9] Audun, it turns out, becomes prudent once he has something to lose. Now as a man of wealth and reputation, he is not about to sell all he hath and put all his eggs in one basket again. He is now lucky in the sense that he is wealthy, but the luck that got him to that point operated just in the nick of time by a rare run of a few well-placed "strokes" of good luck.

When your total net worth is three marks, putting them in one basket may not be all that irrational, like the street person who begs a dollar for coffee but then buys a lottery ticket with it, thereby betting his entire net worth on a 1 in a 150,000,000 long shot. A dollar may be all he has but it is still only a dollar. Granted, three marks could buy Audun quite a bit more than a cup of coffee; something close to that sum bought him a polar bear in Greenland, but once he comes back to Iceland having increased the value of his initial investment by a factor of several hundred, his penchant for non-diversification will undergo a sea change, unless he is really foolish. And Audun is anything but. Part of being lucky means having the ability to know when not to press your luck. You may be forced to rely on your luck in some settings; you may even seek out such settings every once in a while as a test of your luck, but the lucky man will not keep tempting fate as a long-term strategy. Or his luck, so we all believe and they did too, will run out.

There is a time for casting bread upon the waters, a time for considering the lilies of the field, a time for selling all one has and buying a pearl of price, but Jesus is speaking figuratively, though he is serious about giving to the poor. In the miserable cold north, the polar bears are real, the rapacious kings are too, and the poor are not beggars in the street, but your own mother. Practicality is the best bet in the long run. Audun knows that very well.

---

[9] *Egils saga*, ch. 38.

Audun is unthreatening to the kings and no small portion of his luck seems to be owing to that. His luck can thus be counted a virtue by the kings and by himself as well. His luck makes him rich, which remember, is what the word *auð*, the first element of his name, also meant. Under other circumstances, his wealth, his good luck that is, could have, with the slightest twist in the eye of a Harald, been the cause of bad luck. He might not have been as ignorable if he had stuck around, rich. It might have been a good thing he headed back to Iceland, hearing his mother calling, when he did.

When a king makes someone rich or raises someone from low to high estate he may expect loyalty but get rather more than he bargained for. The upstart might become so wealthy as to show the king up; he might be able to afford a body of retainers more numerous than the king can afford, as did Thorolf Kveldulfsson in *Egils saga* to his ultimate misfortune, or he might press his luck in smaller ways, as Aki did, and get dismissed into the darkness after having been raised up into the light. Raising up a poor Icelander is a pretty low-risk way to show your generosity and obviously, as we will discuss under a different heading below, princes cannot repay everyone as richly as they paid Audun or they would soon be paupers. To give well to an occasional Audun, they have also to know how to receive; more precisely, they have to know how to *take* better than they know how to give, or they will not have the wherewithal to put on occasional large shows of magnanimity that will generate good stories and engender a reputation for generosity, if not the virtue itself.

Would Audun's luck have continued to serve him had he stayed in Norway, rich, right under Harald's nose? Would Harald have been able to resist plucking him bare?[1] Consider this rather grim object les-

[1] Much of *Sturlunga saga* shows chieftains and powerful men fleecing poorly defended wealthy farmers, especially by a strategy of supporting doubtful inheritance claims to their estates (e.g., *Sturlu saga*, chs 15–19, 28, 30ff; *Guðmundar saga dýra*, chs 1–3 Helgastaðmál; *Íslendinga saga*, chs 16, 34, in *Sturlunga saga*, 1:229–534, trans. McGrew and Thomas, 1:115–447); but also by forced marriage, by selling protection and other strong-arm tactics (e.g., *Laxdæla saga*, ch. 16; *Guðmundar saga dýra*, ch. 9).

son about the risks of being of low standing and acquiring substantial wealth; it merits a fairly circumstantial account to show what allowances were extended Audun because of his charm, and because he did not stay long enough for his charm to grow stale.[2]

King Harald was paying various visits to feasts in the Upplond region, in effect collecting rents by eating them *in situ*. Attending feasts, visiting people with a hundred armed friends, was one of the ways early medieval kings, and clearly Norwegian kings, collected what we might call rents and taxes, but these rents and taxes were subsumed under the norms of hospitality, using the idiom of gift-exchange that figures as the central theme of our story. The king showed up and ate his host nearly out of house and home and moved on. This way he could keep tabs on the rich and drain their resources.[3] He did not give much advance warning because his visits were also meant moderately to terrorize the big men of the provinces into not getting too many ideas of independence; there was thus an advantage to be had in making visits somewhat randomly. Feasts usually went off as what they purported to be: feasts. But the expense was substantial and there was often a touch of intimidation lurking in them.

The story takes up with Harald making his gastronomical rounds:

> There was a man named Ulf the Wealthy. He owned fourteen or fifteen farms. His wife asked him to invite the king to a feast and said that it would be a more appealing prospect than to be plundered by the king.[4]

Ulf's wife has no illusions that some of Ulf's wealth will have to be shared with the king, especially given his unfortunate nickname; she just thinks it best to have it shared cloaked in the forms of conviviality. The king is going to get his cut in any event. So why not euphemize the transfer of wealth as hospitality, vaguely making it look less involuntary and more gracious than it may in fact be, rather than suffering a transfer that is openly confiscatory with nothing voluntary about it,

---

[2] See the remarks in Andersson and Gade, p. 81.

[3] Compare, however, 12th-century England where food rents had come to be largely commuted into money payments; the enormous logistical problems of the English itinerant court leads Robert Bartlett to conclude that "the foodstuffs were going to court, not the court to the foodstuffs." The Norwegian court however was hardly as rich or as administratively advanced as the English one; see Bartlett, *England under the Norman and Angevin Kings, 1075–1225* (Oxford, 2000), pp. 141–142.

[4] I use Andersson and Gade's translation making some small changes, M ch. 37.

a pure shakedown for "protection"? Ulf follows her advice and invites Harald to his residence, providing sumptuous entertainment.

When at table the king says that it would be fitting for him, Harald, to provide the entertainment by telling a story. Beware the king who plays the minstrel but then, we have had occasion to note that Harald not only liked listening to sagas, and especially his own, he liked composing parts of it himself.[5] Harald then begins a story, composed on the spot, about an upstart slave named Almstein who managed through ability to become the right-hand man of a supposed ancestor of Harald's, King Halfdan. He "offered to collect the land taxes for three summers...but as things turned out, not much of the money got to King Halfdan," recounts Harald.[6] Almstein, in Harald's tale, uses his wealth to good advantage, engineers a coup, and sets himself up as king and immediately cashes in on one of the perks of office, especially indulged in by Scandinavian kings: "He abducted respectable women and kept them in his bed for whatever period of time pleased him and fathered children with them." (Given the sexual habits of Scandinavian kings anyone of uncertain ancestry could play the role of pretender to the throne, claiming his mother or grandmother had slept with a king thus giving him a dose of blood royal.[7])

Later, recounts Harald, Halfdan, who had been in hiding in Sweden, surprises Almstein but spares him his life on condition that he return to his slave status. "I will give you the choice, he says, of returning to your nature and being a slave the rest of your life, along with all who

---

[5] See above pp. 34–35, 66n6.

[6] This illustrates rather pointedly one of the advantages a king gained by being constantly on the move and taxing by eating and drinking. It saved the skimming that his collection agents routinely engaged in as the food moved from the point of production to the point of consumption; see my discussion in *Bloodtaking*, ch. 3; cf. above n3.

[7] Pious King Svein of *Audun's Story* fathered by various unnamed mistresses at least nineteen children. Illegitimacy did not prevent five of his sons from becoming kings of Denmark, one of whom, Knut IV, was sainted. Adam of Bremen, who knew Svein well (Svein addresses him familiarly as "son" [2:41]), greatly relied on the king's knowledge of regional history in composing his *History of the Archbishops of Hamburg-Bremen*. No ingrate, Adam repaid the king by commending Svein's knowledge of letters (3:53), his remarkable ability to remember anything preached to him from the Bible (3:20), and by partly excusing his womanizing—a vice "inborn with that people"—as a function not of evil will but of bad genes (but cf. 3:11). More than a few Norwegian rulers had suspect bloodlines; among the more significant whose claims of royal paternity were doubtful at best: Olaf Tryggvason, Harald Gilli, Sverrir Sigurðarson. Part of Harald's wit in his tale of Almstein is that instead of forging a suspect affiliation to claim a royal title, Harald foists a suspect "royal" filiation on Ulf so he can justify expropriating his wealth.

may be your descendants." Almstein chose life and slavery, and Halfdan gave him a coarse white tunic to signal his slave status.

Harald is just warming up to conclude his tale:

> "The thrall Almstein had many children, and I believe, Ulf," said the king, "that your ancestry is such that Almstein is your grandfather. I, on the other hand, am the grandson of King Halfdan.[8] You and your kinsmen have siphoned off royal property, as is evident here, in the drinking vessels and other precious items. Now, Ulf," said King Harald, "you will take the white tunic that my grandfather Halfdan gave your grandfather Almstein and with it your hereditary title. You shall be a slave forever after."

Harald tells Ulf to put on a white tunic and with high-ridicule presents the tunic as if it were a gift, an award of office: "Now take this tunic that I offered you and which your kinsmen have had, and with the same title and honor they had." Says the saga: "Ulf found the king's wit bitter, but hardly dared do other than to accept the tunic."

Ulf's wife and her kinsmen, undoubtedly freeborn, tell Ulf not to accept the tunic no matter what, for that would lend credence to Harald's suspect tale:

> Then his wife went before the king with a following of relatives and asked that Ulf be forgiven and not be dishonored in this way. The end of it was that the king yielded to their plea and granted Ulf one of the fifteen farms he had owned and did not force him into slavery. But the king confiscated all his drinking vessels and other valuables and took over all his other farms.

The story Harald concocts is one that claims Ulf's wealth is not Ulf's to begin with but was properly part of Harald's inheritance. No story Harald could invent could claim such a "right" to Audun's bear, or even to Audun's haul from Svein once he returned from Denmark, as long as Audun had the social sense to recognize that he owed Harald a generous gift (though funded entirely by Svein) for making his good fortune possible. Might does not completely make right, even for Harald;

---

[8] Harald's father Sigurd Sow is filiated in M ch. 9 and *Heimskringla: Óláfs saga Tryggvasonar*, ch. 60 (ÍF 26), as son of Halfdan, son of Sigurd hrisi, son of Harald Finehair. Sigurd Sow and his ancestors were claimed to have been petty kings of Ringerike. Harald's patrilineage is no less invented than Ulf's, for there is little evidence of Harald's any deeper than the link to his father that can be verified from other sources. There seems to be some textual confusion in the M ms in the early portions of Harald's story of Almstein, in which the scribe should be indicating the death of Sigurd hrisi but writes H. instead, which suggests he mistakenly thought the dying king was Sigurd's father, Harald Finehair.

though he can dispossess a subject not especially well connected, he still feels obliged to justify his claim to do so as a claim of right, as a claim for restitution. And notice that Harald immediately makes concessions to Ulf's wife's kinsmen, further admitting limits on his arbitrariness.

Audun is also reasonably secure when he returns to Norway for he is now an ambassador from Svein and officially a merchant trader, and only very stupid kings would kill such geese who regularly laid them golden eggs.[9] A king will take a cut from merchants in the form of harbor dues, landing fees, and market tolls, but not 14/15 of the value of their capital, as Harald did with Ulf. Harald leaves Ulf, carrying away the title to fourteen farms, drinking vessels, and other valuables (*görsemi*, the same word, recall, used to describe Audun's bear) and is no doubt delighting in making a mockery of the custom of an amiable host sending off an honored departing guest with what the sagas style as "good gifts".[10]

The contrast between Harald's treatment of Ulf and of Audun is not a juxtaposition I am contriving from the substantial array of tales preserved about Harald. The story of Ulf the Wealthy immediately follows *Audun's Story* in the Morkinskinna manuscript. And it is the same playful Harald in both stories. Audun's virtue is to grow rich but then not to stay rich right under Harald's eyes. We may be witnessing the

---

[9] King Sverrir, even in the desperate early stages of his campaigns and raids that ended in his becoming king of Norway, did not plunder merchant vessels; see *Sverris saga*, ch.15: "he would never do harm to merchants, if they knew how to 'value' themselves (*ef þeir kynni meta sik*)." The last clause indicates that if the merchants got uppity, or took sides, or perhaps did not occasionally make gifts, they too might get taxed a little more steeply than was customary; *meta sik* bears the sense too of to tax oneself pecuniarily, as well as the more figurative meaning it has here of knowing one's place.

[10] In a similar vein Harald expropriates the suddenly rich Thorfinn in M ch. 34, two chapters before M's version of *Audun's Story*: "where did that money come from that you have accumulated so quickly?" Thorfinn had arguably misappropriated buried treasure to which Harald felt himself entitled because, presumably, it had been the property of a prior ruler, Jarl Hakon, but the text assumes that it is Hakon's heirs who have the best right, not Harald. Thorfinn tries to keep his find secret, whereas he is legally obliged to publish it (*Gulaþing Law*, §144; the king has a claim only to flotsam, §145; see also §148 and *Frostaþing Law* §16:1, NGL I, pp. 58, 257); trans. Laurence M. Larson, *The Earliest Norwegian Laws, Being the Gulathing Law and the Frostathing Law* (New York, 1935), pp. 124–125, 404. Harald confiscates all of the treasure and also declares "even the property [Thorfinn] had in mercantile ventures" to be forfeit. The text suggests the excessiveness of going after the increase added by Thorfinn's mercantile acumen. As the preceding note indicates even the rapacious Harald needed some justifying cover to plunder a merchant; a thief should not profit from his theft, but kings often profited nicely from punishing thieves. On "good gifts" as a parting ritual of host to guest see pp. 139–140.

uneven transition of a Viking king who is learning to resist the temptation to plunder an Icelander with a bear to a ruler who finds his own subjects easier to fleece in their homes by "taxation"; call it the rise of the administrative state.

But it is not as if the Harald of the Morkinskinna manuscript can always resist fleecing Icelanders bearing gifts either. Right after the tale of Ulf, M tells the story of Brand the Generous, a wealthy Icelander famed for his largesse, as his cognomen indicates. Harald is told by one of his esteemed Icelandic poets, Thjodolf, a friend of Brand's, that no one was better suited to be "king of Iceland than Brand on account of his generosity."[11]

Harald means to put Brand's liberality to the test. He sends Thjodolf to ask Brand for his cloak. Brand, without so much as looking up, says nothing, and lets his cloak fall to the floor. Thjodolf takes it back to Harald and tells him how nonchalantly Brand made the gift. Harald reads this, not incorrectly, as a sign of Brand's high opinion of himself. Thjodolf is next sent to ask for Brand's gold inlaid axe, which he gives, as before, without a word. And so back to Harald for a comment and back to Brand who is now told that the king would like Brand's tunic. Brand again says nothing, rips off one of the tunic's sleeves, keeps that, and tosses the one-sleeved tunic on the floor. Says Harald when he sees the armless tunic: "This man is both clever and magnanimous. It is obvious why he tore off the sleeve. He thinks I have only one arm, one for taking, but none for giving." Harald then sends for Brand whom he honors with gifts.

Like *Audun's Story*, Brand's tale shows Harald bested in a potlatch with a figurative "king", admitting he is overmatched, and concluding matters nicely with no hard feelings and with appropriate closing gifts. All was in good fun, though with Harald fun has an ominous edge. Ulf the Wealthy learns the hard lesson that not all ends happily for people whom Harald decides to joke with. These stories play off (and help establish) Harald's reputation as a taker, but as a taker with a sense of irony. He does in fact recognize some constraints; his irony, his humor, is parasitical on his recognition of them, for he never violates or threatens to violate a norm of justice or reason, without knowing he is gaining a threat advantage for so doing. Even in the case of Ulf, Harald relents enough to let him keep his freedom and one farm;

[11] M ch. 38 (ÍF 4:187–191).

complete dispossession would be neither wise nor appropriate. Harald just wanted to make the story with which he was regaling the company at Ulf's feast have as brutal a black-humored punchline as the fiction he was performing would allow: he wanted the story, literally, no less than the feast, to be at Ulf's expense and to unnerve everyone. Reality admitted a tad less, but only a tad less, highhandedness.

MOTIVES

More than once we have raised questions about Audun's motives, only to postpone them. Students and readers suspect he may be a cunning self-interested operator on the one hand, a holy fool on the other. I, somewhat impatiently, dismissed the view that Audun is merely a holy fool; there is nothing to it. But he is also considerably more than a cunning self-interested operator, though it requires more work to show that view is inadequate and superficial.

Audun has to be moved by something more than self-interest or his story would not have been written, or surely not written the way it was. It would then have been a mere folkloric trickster tale, with which, we already noted, it shares genetic material. To state it directly: if Harald suspected Audun was acting out of naked self-interest, in pursuance of profit maximization, that he was playing him off against Svein, or Svein against him, in order to bid up the price of his bear, that he was only veneering his motives with a patina of naïve charm, Harald would have taken his bear and killed him. If Svein had suspected that Audun was motivated primarily to extract the maximal return for his bear, he would have gotten a pittance compared to what he got, which further confirms that Audun is not being a prig, or insincere, when he enters Svein's accepting the bear on the credit side of his ledger.[1]

Why else drag Aki into the story other than to point out that unabashed pursuit of interest without paying homage to the proper social and moral forms will not get you very far. Even the merchants in this tale modulate profit maximization with generous offers of hospitality; the polar bear hunter defers his pursuit of interest by first acting in what he understands to be in Audun's interest, not his own, by trying to dissuade Audun from buying a bear that it would be imprudent for him to buy. If self-interest is a big part of Audun's motivation then he still manages to use the proper forms so as to disguise it. But Audun is manifestly not a dissimulator. More aptly and plausibly, he has truly transmuted interest into something morally praiseworthy in his world: acting nobly. He believes in the virtue of the proper forms. The author

[1] But see discussion on Audun's being able to afford his sincerity at p. 91.

avoids direct attribution of any of Audun's motives to self-interest and suggests others that are a more substantial part of the mix. And "mix" is the key word, for Audun, no differently than most of us, operates from a motive stew, in which interest, to be sure, is often, but not always, an ingredient. Even in the mercantile world, interest is unlikely to be the *sole* motive driving action. Honor and revenge, envy and hatred, mindless routine, or, as we saw with Thorir and Eirik, friendship and a sense of duty, figure there too.

Consider Audun's various motives. He helps Thorir sell his wares because it seemed like a nice thing to do or because it was *something* to do in his boring world; he buys a polar bear on a whim, a remarkably ill-advised one; he decides to give the bear to Svein without explanation, but both the kings think it a magnanimous and worthy gesture; he goes to Rome, the going itself being its own proper motive according to King Svein. Likewise his return to Iceland to care for his mother is a mix of love, duty, and perhaps homesickness. The motives of Audun that are clearly discernible are all marked as either morally commendable or incomprehensibly reckless.

Yet why introduce the opening detail about Audun's head for debt placement, his head for business, if the author does not mean to tease us, or make us wonder, if Audun is not just "doing business," testing his talent for debt placement on a bigger stage for higher stakes?[2] Was he merely putting on a good show? Cagey operators like Svein and Harald, the latter of whom is in fact portrayed as a classic folkloric trickster in the early chapters of his own saga, are too smart to be gamed or easily faked.[3] Audun must have managed his own talent for business in a way that it operates, if at all, unconsciously or invisibly, not as a motive, but as a resource that assists other proper motives. His head for business surely needn't undo or impermissibly color otherwise

---

[2] That the M and H versions omit this detail makes the question of Audun's motives less complexly a subject of their telling of the story but still do not dispose of the motive question. There remains the puzzle of what makes an Icelander of little account decide to acquire a polar bear with everything he has and give it to King Svein.

[3] M's narration of the young Harald in service to the Byzantine emperor is told as a series of episodes involving aliases, disguises, cheatings, and betrayals; M chs 9–13; *Heimskringla: Haralds saga*, chs 4–15, offers a more muted version, but paints much the same picture. When Harald returns from the east to claim the throne he and Svein formed a short-lived alliance against King Magnus. The moment the alliance ceases to serve Harald's interests he breaks it justifying the breach by staging an assassination attempt on himself which he then blames on Svein; see M ch. 14; also *Heimskringla: Haralds saga*, ch. 22, for a slightly varied account.

proper motives. Still, Audun could not be unaware that in his world Svein had a reputation for generosity, while Harald had one for hard bargaining; that if you wanted to make a haul, best to give to Svein. But did such knowledge make it worth bearding Harald and taking the risks of transport through places Harald himself warned against, "where others who've done no harm can scarcely travel empty-handed" let alone with "such a treasure"?

Is Audun out to make a killing, at such a high risk of being killed? He is a very poor calculator of risk in relation to yield if he thinks this is a good way to get rich quickly and enjoy the proceeds. But by choosing to go abroad as his recompense from Thorir, Audun also reveals he has ambition, for a fairly consistent way in the sagas to gain prestige at home in Iceland is to venture abroad. He seeks to put himself in settings where he might gain the opportunity to make a name for himself, or provide himself enough geographical distance to invent a reputation by cooking up tales that do not beggar enough belief to have people make it worth their while to disbelieve them. It is a noteworthy feature of the sagas that phenomena like flying dragons and fabulous creatures do not normally dwell in Iceland though an occasional Icelander will return from the Baltic claiming to have killed one, which people then take with a grain of salt, while not traveling the entire mental road to complete disbelief.[4]

We can concede Audun his ambition, his head for business and debt placement, and still, as do all the characters in his story, think no rational account can be given of his decision to buy a polar bear and carry it all the way to Denmark to give it to a king. Whatever is moving him, and clearly the desire to do something sagaworthy is one of them, and though getting rich may be his special brand of sagaworthiness, the way he goes about it is simply crazy given the likely yield-to-risk ratio. Sagaworthiness generally demands incurring risks in which success takes guts, talent, as well as a nice assist from luck: it means beating the market, so to speak, and beating it big, or equally,

[4] See, e.g., *Njáls saga*, ch. 119: "One evening, on the coast of Finland, it was Thorkel's turn to fetch water for the crew: he encountered a fabulous monster and was only able to kill it after a long struggle. From there he traveled south to Estonia, where he killed a flying dragon. After that he returned... to Iceland where he had these feats carved above his bed-closet and on a chair in front of his high-seat." Within two pages he will be revealed a coward, not that anyone wouldn't be so revealed when confronted by the estimable Skarphedinn, who never went abroad, and so his witnessed feats at home were rather more credible than Thorkel's exploits overseas.

losing in accordance with the odds, but losing in such grand style that people stand in awe, often for the costs you were able to impose on others before you lost.

And if you claim that Audun's interest, as he conceives it, lies in pursuing sagaworthy deeds, you are invoking self-interest in the tautological way one often sees economists, political scientists, amoralists, and many an undergraduate student invoke it: everything we do, they say, is done because we have decided it to be in our interest—whether such interest is measured in pleasure or dollars—or we wouldn't do it. So you want to buy a polar bear and take it through a warzone to give it away or you like strolling through the streets of the inner city in tweed with a neatly trimmed beard at midnight to prove your left-wing politics is not a sham, well given your ranking of your preferences and desires, who is to question the rationality of such actions? The trouble with this view—and it is hard to underestimate how often people who should know better fall into it—is that it is vacuous. No behavior, no matter how self-destructive, is disqualified: "it is... idle to attribute any importance to a proposition, which, when interpreted, means only that a man had rather do what he had rather do" in Macaulay's mocking of it.[5] Not only "a man". Altruism, some biologists tell us, is about preserving your genes at the expense of the phenotype, so self-interest takes place at the gene level. This may work as a theory for ants and bees but not for the soldier who falls on the grenade to save his platoon mates, half of whom he is not on speaking terms with anyway let alone biologically related to, nor does it explain the complex behavior of a buffalo herd in which individuals put themselves at risk for the baby of one of their unrelated group members,[6] nor does it explain completely the medieval Icelandic emotional preferring of foster-children to one's biological children.[7]

---

[5] Thomas Macaulay, "Mill's Essay on Government," p. 318; quoted in Don Herzog, "Externalities and other Parasites," *University of Chicago Law Review* 67 (2000), 895–924, at p. 898, which see for a general attack on this kind of complacent economism.

[6] See the extraordinary and complexly coordinated rescue by an entire herd of buffalo of a calf in the grip of six lionesses in what is styled as the "Battle at Kruger" http://www.youtube.com/watch?v=LU8DDYz68kM.

[7] Nonetheless, there is a non-vacuous self-interest story that provides some systemic pressure that favors foster children. Foster children have nothing to gain by their foster parents dying since they will not inherit from them, whereas your own children have interests that are not quite congenial to your living a long life. Henry II's longevity was

If the idea of self-interest is to be saved from vacuity, it must be admitted that it is in no one's interest to say No three times, let alone once, to Harald Hardradi's face, unless, perhaps, as in the case of another Harold, you have an army with you. Audun's behavior is often best explained not merely as oblivious to his interest, but as actively seeking to jeopardize it: the unadorned No's to Svein providing the best example, since it would have been so easy to have stated them more politely. There are counter examples, but they are of normal background instrumental rationality of the sort, that if you want coffee, you walk to a convenient shop to buy some or go about brewing it in a reasonably efficient way. But even at that level Audun makes sure to do his business sagaworthily: his destruction of Aki before the king is a case in point.

This is a story of more than just risky business with a happy ending, but of business that no initial fantasies of success, no matter how grandiose, could have contemplated. One can easily fantasize winning the lottery when the jackpot is $240,000,000, and thinking how pleasurable it would be the next day to ask the boss for a raise just so you could tell a tale of what it felt like to hold such a bargaining advantage, but few people short of a brilliant composer of tales, could have foreseen hitting a jackpot as sagaworthily as Audun did. That Audun's propensity to act recklessly does not harm him, but rather seduces powerful actors to further his goals could never have been counted on by Audun.[8] Yet what they find most sagaworthy about him is not that he says No to them, but that he bought a bear with "everything he had". His sagaworthiness is literally *risky business* with business bearing its economic sense of buying goods and transporting them to a distant market for exchange.

So we do have a bit of an interested behavior problem in that he is investing economically, though not rationally, in a polar bear, and it is the initial terms of that investment which intrigue everyone. It is not as if interest is not part of the picture; of course it is. Along with generosity, adventurousness, and the desire to do something worth the

---

eventually the main offense that triggered the revolts of his sons. It is no wonder that an aging father might harbor suspicions about the designs of his children.

[8] The kings' goals range from the serious—making peace, competing at sagaworthiness—to the whimsical: the amusement that this strange but intelligent adventurer offers them.

telling, and these are precisely what make the business riskier than if it were pure business. What delights the kings must be that no one in their right mind would do what Audun is doing simply to make a killing and get rich quick, because in their world as in ours, no rational being would do as Audun did.

Let me add a few more wrinkles to the point alluded to about Audun's head for business and his obvious intelligence. It is likely that Audun had heard stories of grand royal largesse, especially that of Svein; there were folktales in circulation which he also must have heard, one of which we will get to soon, of little people gaining great wealth manipulating gift-exchange games by playing kings off against each other in a generosity competition. Audun knew of the possibility of a richer reward beyond an honorable place to eat and sleep at court, beyond which Svein seemed to have been in no rush to confer upon him. Would such knowledge dispirit Audun, disappoint him in the time gap between Svein's acceptance of the bear and when time came for him to head back to Iceland some months and a trip to Rome later?

It would surely not be in Audun's interest to leak signs of jittery anticipation, eager hopefulness, glum disappointment, or petulant impatience. And he must suppress any indication of anticipating making a big haul. He must either truly be satisfied, or appear to be satisfied, by the mere acceptance of his bear and by being asked to stay on at Svein's court. Perhaps Audun was pleased with nothing more than that; perhaps he had no further fantasies of future reward despite his knowledge that such reward was possible, and even likely, even if it were uncertain as to the exact amount and as to when it would be forthcoming. But should Svein's largesse have stopped with honorable lodging, I suspect there would be no tale, or if there were, it would have been one of Audun the Fool, or of Svein having metamorphosed into Harald.

Might we find here one small part of Audun's motivation to head for Rome, in addition to his piety?[9] Though his pilgrimage surely was not undertaken to prime the king's generosity pump, he might fear he couldn't keep up wearing the proper face, and given his compulsive

[9] Rome provides a different kind of excuse in another saga: the skald and killing machine, Thormod, wryly suggests that the reason that Sighvat, King Olaf the Saint's chief poet, betook himself on a pilgrimage to Rome was to avoid the battle in which Olaf was killed and in which Thormod too will die. Pilgrimages, it is implied, can provide a legitimizing cover for cowardice; *Fóstbræðra saga*, ch. 24 (ÍF 6:266).

truth-telling, such fear might be justified. Dissimulation was not his style. We might posit that self-deception saved him by reducing his expectations to nothing more than what he already received,[10] or that by some miracle his initial satisfaction (and relief) at having the gift of the bear accepted suffered no decay over time. But such ability to stay happy about the delights that emanate from one brief moment of giving a free gift are psychologically beyond most of us, for joy and delight tend to decay, and rather rapidly at that. Post coitem..., etc., is but the most oft-cited version of a truth that is as demoralizingly true in non-erotic domains of satisfaction as in erotic ones. Yet opposing my suggestions in this paragraph is what the first paragraph of the story reveals: that those who part with their goods have to wait to get paid for them. In Audun's world time moved more slowly and sellers and givers must have learned to be patient or be reasonably relaxed about debts owed them, or else they would hardly have been cut out psychologically for that kind of business. Their very anxiety would have put them at a considerable disadvantage.[11]

We can safely surmise that Audun would not have answered Harald's first question about how Svein repaid him quite as sincerely had Svein not rewarded him more lavishly than by merely accepting the bear. Audun can *afford* to be sincere by answering "First, he accepted it," because Svein's mere acceptance is not the end of his story or of his remuneration. Yet at the very moment Audun presents Svein the bear Audun's motives are proper; he is not giving to gain pelf; he is giving in a grandly generous act of perfect freedom. There is nothing the least bit obligatory about Audun's gift. He owes Svein nothing, nor is he his subject; it is a purely initiatory gift, not a payback. And so at the very moment of giving the bear Audun has no problem managing whatever knowledge he has about what presenting a valuable bear to a king famed for generosity might lead to, for he is caught up in the moment having all the right and perfectly avowable motives.

---

[10] Such expectation reduction can be accomplished by the mental mechanism of sour grapes, which is a bit different from the workings of the mind needed to make Audun forget the stories of royal generosity he had heard tell. See generally Jon Elster, *Sour Grapes* (Cambridge, 1983).

[11] See the example of the impatient Norwegian merchant in *Vápnfirðinga saga*, ch. 4, above p. 24n4.

Audun is also aware of the game between the kings in which he is conscripted to play the role of a deniable emissary. He understands the significance of Harald's letting him go when Harald lets him go, and the significance of Svein's gift of the arm ring when it is made, though we must wait until the sublime ending to see how perfectly he has understood his role. There are no open avowals of motive except ones that are in accord with the rules of propriety, obligation, and gratitude, of repayment of favors and gifts; and the story gets its edge because it proves these avowals to be sincere.

Even Harald and Svein, whose game is purely competitive, acknowledge fine action as the motive of the other, not interest, and it is clear that they mean what they say. Harald is direct about his estimation of Svein's magnanimity: "There are few like King Svein, though we haven't gotten along." And Svein does not see grounds for suspicion in Harald's letting Audun go, but nobility and generous action. Harald is "distinguished", "highborn", a man of standing who has done both Audun and himself a kindness. Sure, this is the stuff of mutual congratulation as a form of self-congratulation, kings puffing each other up, sustaining their "class interests"; but it reflects real admiration each of the other, as well as their recognition of the special intelligence of this enterprising Icelander.

Harald and Svein are engaged not just in the competition of war, but also in who can look the best in this story, with "best" being awarded for generosity, nobility of spirit, for wit, intelligence, and delicacy. It is a competition in which acting well across a range of values is *the* game; it is more than a potlatch to see who could give Audun the most. To act well, one has to manifest proper sentiments and proper motives, because those too are part of the act. Is it in their interest so to behave? Yes, but it is not interest narrowly conceived that is moving them.

Audun is no self-torturer regarding the propriety of his motives; even his trip to Rome is treated as a simple act of piety, not as a morbid desire to seek absolution for his sins or sinful desires. Nor do Svein, Audun, or the author see Audun's getting rich in this world as anything to trouble a conscience. A real operator, a real calculator, an economist might say, would do exactly as Audun did; he would know where to park any knowledge that would interfere with having proper motives because such parking was what his interest demanded. Assume for a second that this is not the usual tautology that all action is interested no matter what appearances to the contrary might suggest. This is precisely the kind of calculating the story—in the cagey, comically wise, and intelligently reticent way it deals with motive—suggests won't work. Proper motives, avowable motives, must be the main ingredients of the motivational stew. That, again, is what it means to put on a good show. *Audun's Story* is a handbook on how to play the gift game exactly right, not by gaming it, but by performing well, because, to apply an image from Yeats, there is no way to tell the dancer from the dance. The good performance is not *merely* a good performance but rather makes the performer who and what he purports to *be*.[12]

Except for Aki's, calculation in the story must be inferred, guessed at, supposed; it is suggested by the manifest intelligence of the actors and, above all, by the mutual recognition at the end of what debts had been incurred and needed to be discharged; clearly they are keeping track of debts and favors. Do not get me wrong. The story is not just a feel-good tale: it is a story of politics and economics too. But what makes the story so powerful is precisely the narrator's and the main actors' delicacy about keeping track of their debts.

Motives are rendered either as proper or as ambiguous enough to pass for proper. The story treats the discerning of motive in others the way we treat it in real life: as guesses varying from very educated and informed; to conventional assumptions given the accompanying words, actions, and facial expressions; to shots in the dark, now privileging the dominance of one motive, now the other, now concocting motive stews which have no particular name, but that we indicate roughly by invoking the name of the person as a character likely to be motivated in certain kinds of ways: "well you know, that's Harald for you," "that's just like Audun, isn't it?" That "just like Audun" is one of the names we give to a probabilistic set of motives we have no better or more refined vocabulary to get at. And surprisingly normal people tend to be good enough at discerning another's motives to manage reasonably well and not get killed or swindled too often. We might not manage as daringly or as well as Audun, but that is why he has a story named after him, and we don't.

Audun's Story traces its descent nonetheless, as we have noted, to classic trickster tales, so it is hard to sneer at those who might claim that there is strategically interested behavior going on. There is thus more

[12] See Erving Goffman, *The Presentation of Self in Everyday Life* (New York, 1959), p. 75, for performing as *being*: "to *be* a given kind of person, then, is not merely to possess the required attributes, but also to sustain the standards of conduct and appearance that one's social grouping attaches thereto."

literary/folkloric warrant than philosophical, biological, or psychological justification for believing that Audun is a man out to make the biggest killing he can. Nor is the author unaware of the depth his tale gains by playing off expectations its trickster ancestry raises. But *Audun's Story* has so transcended the trickster genre from which it derives as not to be that kind of story.

GAMING THE SYSTEM: *GIFT-REF*

There is however such a story. A certain Jarl Neri refuses to accept gifts because he cannot bear parting with his own goods to repay them. Once, against his practice, he accepts an ox from a troubled boy named Ref and though he cannot suffer repaying the ox out of his own goods he still feels obliged to make some repayment. He requites Ref with shrewd advice about how to make a killing by trading up gifts of increasing value by involving kings in a generosity competition. By the time it is over Ref is a jarl married to a king's daughter. *Gift-Ref's Saga*[1] is a pure folk tale; it is combined with several folkloric tales to make up what is called *Gautreks saga.*

King Gautrek has lost his beloved queen some time before and is so depressed and listless that he fills his days sitting on her grave mound flying his hawk. The hawk has less staying power than the king and tires each day, whereupon the king throws things at the bird to get it to take flight again. Jarl Neri gives Ref a whetstone of miniscule value and tells Ref to wait until the king is groping about behind him for something to throw at the bird and then put the whetstone in his hand. Ref duly carries out the instructions; Gautrek does not bother to look around to see who handed him the stone, but since he hits the bird with it, and experiences a brief surge of pleasure, he hands back a gold arm-ring to Ref, again without so much as turning his head to see to whom he is giving the ring.

Neri next advises Ref to give the ring to King Ælla of England. This is the first of several re-givings and it sets up the formula to be followed in subsequent encounters with a succession of kings. King Ælla asks who gave Ref the ring and what Ref had given to gain such

[1] On the textual history of *Gautreks saga* see Wilhelm Ranisch, ed., *Die Gautrekssaga in zwei Fassungen*, Palaestra, XI (Berlin, 1900); see also Bruce Lincoln, *Theorizing Myth: Narrative, Ideology, and Scholarship* (Chicago, 1999), p. 280nn6, 12. A more conveniently accessible Norse edition can be found in *Fornaldarsögur Norðurlanda*, ed. Guðni Jónsson (Reykjavík, 1954), 4 vols, 4:1–50, *Gjafa-Refs saga* at pp. 36–50; trans. Hermann Pálsson and Paul Edwards, *Gautrek's Saga and other medieval tales* (New York, 1968), pp. 43–53. The story of Ref exists in two versions; I follow the younger one here, but any points I am making would not differ were I to use the older version. *Gift-Ref* and its economic opportunism are discussed in Lincoln, pp. 181–182.

a prize as a countergift. Once informed that it was a mere whetstone, the king remarks on the boundless generosity of King Gautrek and confesses that nothing he could repay Ref could match that. In fact, though, the king does match and even exceed the market value of the ring with his countergifts, though he fails by his own confession to match Gautrek, because he cannot match the multiples of the ring-to-whetstone ratio.[2]

By the time Ref arrives in Denmark to trade up part of what the English king gave him, he is already famous and has acquired a nickname: Gift-Ref. Ref's racket is no secret (Ref, it so happens, is the Norse word for fox)[3]. Everyone knows after his first two moves exactly what is going on: Ref is in the business of trading up and re-gifting royal gifts. What makes it a fairy tale is that the kings go along with it. No deep politics inform their competition; it seems they have a bemused sense that they have been cast as character actors in a trickster tale and they will play their parts without complaint. Yet even in tales like this there are some nontrivial things that shed light on social practices and on ideas of value.

The sources of increasing value of Ref's gifts track some of those noted in *Audun's Story*, but not completely. At each subsequent gift, the king who is about to receive a gift from Ref asks about the chain of exchanges that constitute the history of the object being handed to him. The length of the chain itself, each link representing a transaction with a king, increases the value of the final link independently of any market value the actual gift handed over would have if it were traded at a fair near the harbor. Like the shells in Micronesian kula exchange, and like Audun's polar bear, the gifts, in addition to being gifts of objects, are also gifts of the story that accompanies the objects and which give them their value in this restricted exchange system. The final gift to the Swedish king thus has within it a story that includes King Gautrek, Ælla (the English king)[4] and Hrolf Kraki (the legendary Danish king).

---

[2] Such folkloric tales are now enacted on the internet in a trading-up game: see http://oneredpaperclip.blogspot.com/ in which a red paper clip initiates a series of trades that fourteen moves later ends with a modest house in Kipling, Saskatchewan.

[3] In Old Norse too the fox represented cunning and slyness.

[4] Unlike the other legendary kings of the tale Ælla was in fact a king of Northumbria. In one Norse tale he is noted for having his corpse mutilated by carving him up as a "blood eagle." According to the *Anglo-Saxon Chronicle* Ælla was killed by Vikings in 867, though whether he suffered the blood eagle, or even whether the blood eagle

Not all the value in gift exchange is mystically constructed in the Maussian style from an inability to keep persons and things separate, so that some part of the persons of the kings who participated in the chain is what drives up the value of the objects given, as Harald's personhood and Audun's moral qualities add value to the bear. The kings themselves tell a different story about measuring value in this game. What they claim sets the standard, a standard they admit they cannot match, is not how much one obtains in absolute "dollars" in each exchange, but what the *percentage* increase was of countergift to gift (this is hardly irrational, it is economic rationality itself: it is how return on an investment is measured for bonds, stocks, merchandise, etc., in financial transactions today).

But why should the kings use that standard when it puts them in a Ponzi scheme of exponentially increasing values? Because it is a fairy tale is the sensible answer. No one can reward Ref at the *rate* Gautrek did by repaying a whetstone with a gold arm-ring. Nor, to their credit, do the kings bankrupt themselves trying. Even in a fairy tale kings mind their property better than the crazed Gautrek does. But the tale also shows that even in a fairy tale gaming the system depends on the kings being willing to be openly gamed from time to time. "Social life would not last long if men were not taken in by each other," says La Rochefoucauld (Maxim 87).[5] There is an obligation to be taken in, or if not taken in, to play as if one were taken in, within limits to be sure. The kings, though, believe in these displays and believe in a norm of reciprocity, and mean to sustain a world in which they can be figures in a fantasy like this one. But put Ref in the real world and he is more likely to end up cast out among the Aki's of the world, than rewarded in the manner of Audun, for unlike Audun, his opportunism is openly admitted, and Ref means to stick around and become one of the club.[6]

Note too that it is also easy for the kings to concede the magnanimity prize to the depressed and elderly Gautrek because he is presently not

---

was not itself a poetic invention, is a cause for dispute; see *Ragnarssonar þáttr*, ch. 3, in *Fornaldarsögur Norðurlanda*, 1:298. For a debunking of the blood eagle see Roberta Frank, "Viking Atrocity and Skaldic Verse: The Rite of the Blood-Eagle," *English Historical Review*, 99 (1984), 332–343.

[5] See also Maxim 282.

[6] Ref returns to Gautrek's kingdom with the Swedish king's army, the loan of which he got as a countergift and, with Neri doing the negotiating, he extorts a jarldom and a daughter from the mourning king.

much of a threat sitting on his mound throwing stones at his hawk. For in their world it is always the case that when kings give gifts it is the stuff of politics, whether it be by rewarding a skald or a retainer, or by sending peace feelers to other kings as in *Beowulf* and *Audun's Story*. The effect of achieving a reputation for magnanimity is to draw skalds who will further burnish one's reputation and draw retainers who will provide the force necessary to acquire the very pelf needed to reward them. And it is not as if these retainers and skalds appear from nowhere, rather they are pried away from the kings and magnates one is competing with and will soon be fighting against again. For if there is one thing in especial that is the signature of medieval politics from a lowly archer to a baron or even a king, it is side-switching. Alliances and groups were constantly forming, splitting, and reforming, and faithfulness, though often invoked as a virtue, had a relatively short half-life.

REGIVING AND RECLAIMING GIFTS

Audun's Story depends on the richly textured and complex practices of gift exchange. I have written about this before in both Norse and modern contexts and the anthropological literature on the topic is vast.[1] But the saga materials are especially fertile ground, as rich as any in the standard ethnographic accounts. The norm of reciprocity is more than morally and socially operative in the Norse world. The obligation to return a gift is in some settings legally enforceable. Let me get at this by treating of the respect one owes a gift received and a corollary, the circumstances under which one might undo a gift given, either because one regrets having given it, or because it has not been adequately recompensed.

Suppose after having received the parting cloak and sword from King Harald, Audun gave them to someone else before he got on his ship to sail back to Iceland. What are the rules regarding gifts one receives beside the obvious one of recompense? Can you give them away? If so, must you hide what you have done from the original giver? Or does it depend on whom you give it to, or the quality of your excuses for so doing? Or is there an informal statute of limitations, after which any right the original giver has to feel wronged, or burden you with guilt, for undervaluing his gifts rightly expires? Even an heirloom might exhaust its sacredness, as did the relics of various saints that ceased working miracles. Then too there is the seeming paradox that makes us feel more obliged, at times, to keep a gift we loathe, than one we love. More than a few of us have parked in the attic gifts we find so tasteless that we would never display them or dare be seen using them, but that we believe we cannot throw or give away without offending the furies, or some not-so-distant relative.

Can the giver ask for his gifts back if you try to give them away? Might he be able to sue to recover them? Does it matter whether the gift was an initiatory gift, the one that started it all, or whether it was a payback for a prior gift, with the latter entitled to lesser dignity, or whether it was a closing gift meant to bring the cycle of exchanges to an

[1] Miller, *Bloodtaking*, ch. 3; *Humiliation* (Ithaca, NY, 1993), ch. 1.

end? Are there different rules for different kinds of gifts, a sword playing by one rule, a cloak or an ox or an axe by another? And does it matter who it was who gave them, and who it was who received them?

It would be a mistake ever to think that such questions have easy answers, for each situation will present its own circumstances that might alter what counts as a violation of proper behavior or what can be excused or understood as an imaginative and justifiable response to a special situation. But there are tendencies which can at times be stated as if they were hard and fast rules. Such rules often appear as proverbs in all cultures and sometimes in the Norse world as laws.

Audun's Story puts the issue of re-gifting a gift squarely in play. The sublimity of the ending depends on doing just that, as Audun gives to Harald the arm-ring that Svein gave to him, and we have already discussed how Svein explicitly gave more than permission to pass it on, but subtly ordered that it be done, limiting Audun's title in the ring rather severely.

Another tale adds significant complexity to the various expectations and rights the original giver might think to retain in his gift, at least when that giver is a king. The tale involves Brand the Generous, whom we met a short time ago, King Olaf the Saint, and Isleif Gizurarson, the same who made a gift of a polar bear to the German emperor in 1055.[2] The events in the brief vignette that follow occurred some three decades earlier when Isleif was a young priest.

Isleif had just arrived in Norway from Germany where he had been studying. Brand was in attendance on King Olaf at the time. Olaf held Brand in high esteem and as an indication of it gave Brand a fine scarlet cloak lined with gray fur. Then this:

> Brand ran into Isleif in town, and they were each delighted to see the other. Isleif was a priest at the time and quite poor when he arrived from the south.
>
> Brand said, "Accept from me this cloak the king gave me."
>
> He said, "You are as generous spirited as ever; I will accept it with pleasure."
>
> Later in the holiday when Brand was eating with the king, the king looked at him and said, "Brand, why aren't you wearing the cloak I gave you?"
>
> He said, "My lord, I gave it to a certain priest."

[2] See p. 20.

The king said, "I want to see the priest to see if I will judge it excusable that you have so quickly dealt away a king's gift."

People were rather amazed that Brand would treat such a person's gift so cavalierly. And when on their way to a church-meeting Brand said to the king: "My lord, there's the priest, next to the church; he is wearing the cloak."

The king looked at the priest and said, "We are changing course, Brand, because now I want to give him the cloak. Call the priest over to me."

Brand said he would do so.

Isleif then approached the king and greeted him. The king accepted the greeting with pleasure and said, "That cloak, priest, that Brand gave you, I want to give it to you. I will repay Brand its value, because you so please me that I wish to gain the protection of your prayers."

He answered, "My lord, I thought this gift a splendid one when Brand gave it to me, but it has even greater value coming from you with these words."[3]

The king believes he retains a right to reclaim his gift if it has been "abused" or insufficiently honored, and being a strong king his belief regarding his rights does much to realize those rights. But the king does not go about reclaiming the gift as highhandedly as he might have. He acts with considerable restraint. He thus compensates Brand for its value, presumably the compensation being directed to satisfy two, possibly three, things: any dishonor to Brand by reclaiming it, any return Brand was expecting from Isleif that may now be compromised, or, supposing, as likely, the cloak was a repayment for gifts Brand had previously made to Olaf, a new discharge of that debt.

This episode is more complex than it seems though. Is Brand's act of generosity wiped off the slate? Does Isleif, in other words, still have to repay Brand? In support of Isleif's continuing obligation to Brand, hasn't the king actually ratified or confirmed Brand's gift by remaking it to the same beneficiary? How different is that from Svein giving pointed permission to Audun to regift the arm-ring to Harald? In each case the original giver is okaying the transfer, one before it takes place, one after it took place. It thus does not appear that Isleif handed the cloak back to Olaf so that Olaf could physically hand it back to Isleif. The story is unlikely to have omitted such a significant act had it occurred. The cloak stays on Isleif by Brand's hand.

[3] *Bishop Isleif's Story* (*Ísleifs þáttr byskups*, ÍF 16:335–336); it is found in F's version of *Óláfs saga helga*.

Relevant law

The Icelandic laws, in part, treat certain rights of reclamation of gifts as follows:

> A). No one has the right to cancel a gift he has made. If the receiver promises a return for the gift, the giver has the right to claim such a sum as is decided by a verdict of neighbors on the content of his promises...
>
> B). If a man makes a gift worth twelve ounce-units or more to someone to whom he owes no return either for assistance or for gifts and if, further, the gift is not returned to half its value, then he has the right to claim his gift if the other dies.[4]

The first sentence of A says one cannot take back a gift. Then come the qualifications. A giver can sue and collect on any promise made to him to make a return, and in paragraph B, even in the absence of a promise he has a right to reclaim the thing itself from the recipient's heirs, if the recipient did not make at least a .5 payback. The law backs the deep cultural commitment to reciprocating a gift, especially when the gift reaches amounts of non-trivial value.

In paragraph A, the giver cannot retake the underappreciated gift itself, but he can get the value of any promise in money compensation if a promise were made. These must be gifts worth less than twelve ounce-units; those above that amount, dealt with in B, have a fairly strong right of reclamation triggered by ingratitude, or by repayment on the cheap. Even paragraph A, despite its "no one has the right to cancel a gift he has made", has the look of trying to limit, and not all that much, what seems to have been a rather insistent expectation on the part of the giver to be able to take back a gift if he did not get a return gift. Or were these provisions—which seem to turn gifts into loans—meant to govern situations where there was some understanding

---

[4] *Grágás* Ia 247, II 84–85. The events of the passage I am discussing took place in Norway where *Grágás* did not govern. The laws of the Norwegian Gulaþing, in a passage that is rather obscure, give "everyone a right [to recall] a gift unless it has been requited with a better payment; a gift is not requited unless an equal amount is set over against that which was given." But "gifts that the king gives us or that we give to him shall remain valid"; *Gulaþing Law* §129 (NGL I, p. 54; trans. Larson, *The Earliest Norwegian Laws*, pp. 118–119). Larson's translation supplies the "to recall" which seems necessary to make sense of the elliptical Norse; see Karl von Amira's attempt to render the passage in *Nordgermanisches Obligationenrecht*, vol. 2: *Westnordisches Obligationenrecht* (Leipzig, 1895), p. 615.

that the transfer was something less than a gift?[5] It must be that there were gifts and then there were "gifts," the latter employing the sociable diction of gift exchange but understood to be more in the nature of a friendly loan, as from a padrone to his client, who might have been short on fodder or food.

When her kinsman Ingolf gave Steinunn the Old[6] a tract of land, she insisted on giving him a hooded cloak for it because "she wanted to call it a purchase, for it seemed to her that that reduced the risk of its being reclaimed."[7] Steinunn thinks there is a robust right of reclamation, and her tactic of giving an immediate quid pro quo is meant to eliminate it. She fears Ingolf, or more likely his heirs, might take the land back if it is considered a gift and they find the value of her return gifts not up to measure. She wants no talk of gifts; for her it is a purchase and a sale, and that means if not quite a done deal, then one that substantially lowers the risk and rights of reclamation she fears. But this is a land transfer and gifts of land would be expected to come with reversionary strings attached, especially in Norse law.[8]

In Iceland, the heirs retain a right of reclamation should their father give "gifts of friendship" for the purpose of disinheriting them. If the heirs think the motive of the gift-giver is purposely to dispossess them, they can bring suit against him and have him forfeit the management of his property as well as be subject to lesser outlawry; the recipients

[5] See von Amira, 2:616–620 *passim*, where the distinction between contract and gift pretty near collapses; see the discussion of von Amira's position by Beate Wagner-Hasel, "Egoistic Exchange and Altruistic Gift: On the Roots of Marcel Mauss's Theory of the Gift," in Algazi et al., pp. 141–171, at pp. 152–153.

[6] "Old" as a cognomen does not refer to Steinunn's age but is meant to place her genealogically in the manner Senior does among us, and would most likely have been attached to her several generations after her death.

[7] The transfer took place in the settlement period in the late 9th and early 10th centuries and is preserved in a 13th-century account in *Landnámabók*, S 394 (ÍF 1:392); cited also in von Amira, 2:615–616. Though its reliability as a statement of late 9th-century practice can be doubted, as a substantive matter it rings true for any number of transactions in various places at various times.

[8] A more forceful right of reclamation would also include sales of patrimony within its ambit, not just gifts of it, as in Norwegian *óðal* land, and in Iceland in a ward's option right to repurchase lands sold by his guardian that had been part of his deceased ancestor's estate; see *Grágás* Ib 76–79, and the considerably more detailed section in II 410–418; *Gulaþing Law* §§265–294 (NGL I, pp. 86–96). Any right of Ingolf's heirs to reclaim the land he transferred to Steinunn is uncertain. Ingolf was the first settler in Iceland. He was passing on previously unowned land, and at this early stage whether any Norwegian-style buy-back rights would attach to his land-claim to the benefit of his kin would be, I imagine, open to dispute.

of these friendship gifts are also punishable with lesser outlawry and the gifts are revoked.[9]

And should father try to follow the Gospel and give all he has to the poor, the heirs can set that aside. Father is limited to a gift of ten percent of his net worth—called the great tithe—once in his lifetime "for the good of his soul," but not more unless he gets the heirs to join in the gift.[10] Skirting the interest of the heirs in the property one wishes to give away may account for the fact that Brand the Generous is generous abroad, far away from the jealous eye of kinsmen out to make sure their "expectations" remain great expectations and who do quite trust the value of any returns for gifts made to the Church or to kings.

The charitable giver himself can recover gifts he made to a pauper:

> When a man gives hospitality to someone for God's sake and it is not his place to maintain him and the dependent dies and it turns out that he had property to leave, then the man who housed him has the right to take it and not the heirs.[11]

---

[9] *Grágás* Ia 247, II 85. A man has a right to give goods of twelve ounce-units to an illegitimate child without getting the heirs' consent; this provision provides the background to a well-known episode in *Laxdæla saga* (ch. 26) where a father gets the consent of his legitimate sons for a gift of twelve ounces to his favorite child, the illegitimate Olaf, but then tricks the heirs by making it twelve ounces of gold, rather the twelve legal ounces based on the *vaðmál*-to-silver standard. For cases of *arfskot* or inheritance-fraud, see, e.g., *Eyrbyggja saga*, chs 31–35; *Sturlu saga*, ch. 26; *Íslendinga saga*, ch. 148.

[10] *Grágás* Ia 246–247, II 84. Compare the looser norms more favorable to the church in 12th-century Normandy and England where gifts of inheritance were limited to "reasonable" amounts, which could be as high as a third; see John Hudson, *Land, Law, and Lordship in Anglo-Norman England* (Oxford, 1994), pp. 182–183.

[11] *Grágás* Ia 230, II 99. Compare *Leges Henrici Primi* §88:15, ed. and trans. L.J. Downer (Oxford, 1972), pp. 274–277. There, a dispute is envisaged between the heirs of a man (N) who had been abandoned by those same heirs and someone, most likely a remoter kinsman, who cared for N, for which generosity N rewarded his benefactor by adopting him "as a son," thus disinheriting the heirs. The case is to be settled by "wise men in accordance with the circumstances." John Hudson notes that there is no written source behind the provision and also that, in the English setting, displacing closer blood by means of adoption was not common (*Land, Law, and Lordship in Anglo-Norman England*, p. 123). Might we not see in the *Leges* some connection to the Scandinavian rules regarding the obligation to sustain poor kin (such as the *Grágás* provision to which this note is attached and those discussed in the following section in the text), which allow volunteers to recover their charitable gifts should the recipient of that charity die with assets, or come into property later? The "wise men" in the *Leges* provision would thus indicate those people in the community who were known to be good at appraising land and goods, sharing a talent with those men of the vill who were selected to serve as informants for the Domesday commissioners. The reason the *Leges* provision is not explicit as to who has the right to the estate is because such determination must

What would Jesus do with our pious almsgiver who undertakes out of pure charity to support a poor man but then reclaims his charity later from the pauper's heirs? Icelandic law recognized a formal procedure of selling one's inheritance in return for maintenance, but it appears in the case of the pious benefactor that even in the absence of such a contract the law will read one in if the recipient of charity happens to die with assets.[12] Would the pious donor excuse his reclaiming his gift as the good fortune that God promised from a properly motivated casting of one's bread upon the waters, even when he must *sue* to get his return? Does interest have to reassert itself in such a contentious form when one comes to regret one's former charitableness? But regretting his charity may not be his motive at all. Consider the following.

Serious scarcity, self-interest, and Audun's mother

The law allowing a man who shows hospitality to the poor to recover his outlay needs to be understood against a backdrop of conditions of scarcity that boggle the mind. Every calorie counted then, not in the way they count for us, at the high end, but at the low end. Though this law appears in the inheritance section of the codex of laws, it best fits with the policies of the section which deals with enforcing upon kin the obligation to take care of their legal dependents, which include in some circumstances kin as remote as fourth cousins.[13] A law in the dependents' section, much like the law allowing the charitable volunteer

---

await the evaluation of the charitable outlay and other "circumstances" which might include a penalty charged against the abandoning heirs unless they could plead and prove their own poverty as an excuse; see also p. 16 above.

[12] Such an inheritance sale must be made with the consent of those who would qualify as the heirs at the time of the transfer; *Grágás* Ia 236. If it turns out that other people than those who consented to the sale accede to heirship at the time of the inheritance seller's death the sale is voided, though the purchaser of the inheritance gets to recover his purchase price with interest. And in what is marked as a "new law" in both main mss of the laws, it is provided that an inheritance sale could also be set aside by the heirs of either party if it was deemed "unfair," that is, if the outlay needed to support the dependent seller of the inheritance had less value than the inheritance he sold or, reciprocally, if it turned out that the cost of maintenance exceeded the value of the inheritance; *Grágás* Ia 237–238. The provision quoted on p. 104 shows the laws concerned also to protect the assets of the provider of maintenance, though he acted out of charity, if it turns out that the dependent provided for either came into some property later, or had assets that could have paid or contributed to the costs of maintaining him at the time the charity was given.

[13] *Grágás* Ib 3–28, II 103–151; see also *Sturlu saga*, ch. 16, re claim of Alf.

to recover his gifts just discussed, allows anyone who is *obliged* to take in a poor dependent kinsman to recover his costs from that dependent's closer kin should these closer kin later acquire assets.

Suppose Thorstein, Audun's wealthy kinsman with whom he lives, undertakes to support Audun's mother when Audun is abroad because, assuming further, Audun could not afford to or stayed abroad at Svein's court for more than three years. When Audun comes back rich, Thorstein's outlay for Audun's mother is recoverable against Audun, or for that matter against his mother, should she inherit assets from Audun or another relative. Coming into wealth after the fact means you have to discharge all the obligations you avoided by truthfully pleading poverty earlier. Nor would Thorstein lose his right to recover for the outlay he made for Audun's mother because he said something like, "don't worry Audun, I will provide for your mother while you are gone." Sudden good fortune means the *gifts* given to support you, or to those who would have been charges upon you had you the means to support them at the time, are transformed into *loans* that can be sued on if you do not pay them back now that you have the means.[14]

Such laws bring home the harsh realities that transform the saga gift-exchange culture into anything but one that can be romanticized on account of its using the idiom of gifts to do a lot of work that insurance or the government does for us. And selfish interest in this world is something that the laws allow to be asserted without shame, as here, to recover gifts made disinterestedly at a prior time. Genuinely generous motives thus are seen to be transmuted by time and context, reinterpreted, and overridden, depending on the wealth of the individuals involved and the rise and fall of their fortunes. But that does not mean the charitable outlay, the hospitality, was a sham or an exercise in self-deception when it was given.

There may be utilitarian arguments that can justify the stricture that might sadden Jesus when it allows the charitable volunteer to recover his charity. The provision may actually make more giving possible than would occur without it. It gets assets back into the hands of people who have already demonstrated their willingness to care for "incapable people", which is how the Icelandic term for dependents (*ómagar*) can

---

[14] *Grágás* Ib 10; see also II 136. These provisions differ from the one discussed on p. 102 in that they divide liability for repayment differently as between the actual beneficiary of the largesse and his heirs; see also Ib 27; also Ia 246–247, II 83–85 discussed in part above, pp. 102–103.

be literally translated. Yet one can also see in provisions like this the desperate fear the incapable poor—too old or too young or too ill to work—generated in those people who were managing to get by, but not with very large margins for error.

In this regard it is of some interest that Audun's kinsman, the prosperous Thorstein, who has relatively generous margins for error—his farm, remember, offered the best accommodation for the Norwegian merchant Thorir—did not volunteer to help sustain Audun's mother,[15] nor did Audun think that if he did not get back in three years that Thorstein would undertake to support her, though Audun and he were clearly on good terms. Audun may be exaggerating in order to give Svein an excuse he will accept, but he paints for Svein what must have been an unnervingly plausible image of his mother, homeless, begging house to house. Audun is not banking, in any event, on Thorstein's charity to sustain his mother, even though Thorstein has the means.

This is another gentle reminder that the gift exchanges that take place at the high end of the social order in *Audun's Story*, in formal ritualized gestures of giving and repaying, are rather different from the watchful needy world of taking care of people who are a drain on the scarce resources of others, a world in which people must have devoted a considerable portion of their memories to keeping track of who owed them what, and in resource poor Iceland such people were not contemptible villeins, but respectable farmers. So if dependent paupers later came into funds after having earlier benefited from charity, who can blame the shift in motive that turns the former giver of charity into a plaintiff in a lawsuit to recover the cost of his kindness, if the beneficiary of his charity happens to have a short memory?

In the gift vs. in on the gift

Most gifts come with strings attached. This is hardly news to anyone. But some strings are legalized, some strings tug at the heart by raising sentiments of obligation—from gratitude to feelings of oppression—and some strings are quite thin, both legally and morally. Such are those

[15] She may not be a blood relative of Thorstein who might be related to Audun on Audun's paternal side. If that were the case, Thorstein would not be obliged to maintain her beyond the period Audun had funded.

that let you reclaim a cloak if the giver regives it, especially, if as seems likely, the gift is less an initiatory gift, than a recompense, a countergift to Brand for gifts Olaf had already received from him.

What does Olaf's reclamation, a half-hearted reclamation at that, add to the gift? Olaf, it seems, is not satisfied to know that in Maussian theory his spirit haunts the gift so that it will always seek to return to its original home. This gift is not coming back unless Olaf reclaims it, and moreover he only wants it back to give it away again, and this time really for good. Olaf's actions can be read to show a distinction that matters greatly to him between his being *in* the gift and his being *in on* the gift. When Brand gives the "king's gift" to Isleif—"accept from me this cloak the king gave me"—the generosity of Brand that Isleif remarks upon is a reference to the value of the gift not only as a splendid cloak, but as one that Brand got from King Olaf. Olaf is already *in* the gift to Isleif, as Brand takes care to inform him when he gives it to him: "this cloak the king gave me."

Gifts from kings and other high-ranking people get their own special nomenclature in Old Norse; the object gets a name by adding *naut* (meaning, gift, present) to the genitive of the name or title of the giver, as long as the giver is of a notable rank: Olaf's-naut, king's-naut, jarl's-naut, Hakon's-naut. Not just any object merits such personification. Cloaks, swords, spears, axes, rings qualify, an occasional ship, and that's about it. The gifts that are *naut*s thus tend to have something inherently personal about them, and are generally portable, and worn, or make one portable, like a ship.[16] They may not be exactly imbued with the soul of the giver but they bear his name or title whether gifted down the line or not. But, though obvious, it still needs to be noted: it is not the original giver who gives these *nauts* their name, but the recipient. And he does so to indicate the value he puts on it, or, more accurately, to indicate the value he expects envious others to put on it, which then will make up most of its value to him.[17]

---

[16] See the cloak, sword, and ring, variously *konungsnaut*, *jarlsnaut*, and *Sigvaldanaut* in *Hallfreðar saga*, chs 6, 9–10. Some objects were given names independently of whether they were gifts. As we still do, so did they name ships. They also named pet weapons, and of course pet animals.

[17] A "naut"-gift is not going to come back home, despite all the anthropological writing on the Maori *hau*, the spirit of the giver seeking to bring the gift back home. Some objects alienated via gift or sale really are meant to come back home: e.g., land that is subject to *óðal* right. The spirit imbuing other objects, a gift of more moveable property for instance, is willing to settle for some kind of equivalent return. The dif-

But being already *in* the gift is not good enough for Olaf. He wants to be *in on* the gift as well and for that, he believes, his personhood imbuing the object is not enough. He wants to be seen as the presenter to this particular recipient, not just as the most notable link in the cloak's chain of title—the presenter of its presenter. *Audun's Story* shows that the directness of presenting can be finessed, as when Harald gets in on

ferent expectations—return of the thing itself vs. substitutional return—maps onto the difference in legal remedies of a right to recover the actual object (as when one sues a thief who still retains the goods) vs. damages (as when one sues the thief who already has sold the stolen property); in the idiom of the common law forms of action, it is the difference between replevin and trover. There is some rather loose use of the notion of the "inalienability" of the gift in the literature. See, e.g., Annette B. Weiner's *Inalienable Possessions: The Paradox of Keeping-While-Giving* (Berkeley, 1992). Weiner's own ethnographic materials show the possession of valued inalienable objects being transferred all the time. "Inalienable" thus becomes a way of indicating those goods one values greatly and does not want to part with, but which are precisely the goods others will seek to extract by gift, theft, or plunder and which the owner may be forced to sell in dire straits if he has no other assets. The ability to rent, loan, give, or sell these objects shows that whatever "inalienability" means in some kinds of Maussian discourse it does not mean possession (even ownership) cannot be transferred. Depending on the object, what the giver or his heir retains is more in the nature of a reversion or option and sometimes nothing more forceful than a longing and regret, at best a name attached to the object, as when the used book you buy bears the signature of a prior owner whom you do not know and who you suspect, given the age of the book, the style of the hand, and fading of the ink, is dead (there is often a strange melancholic evocativeness in those signatures). This is a far cry from the inalienability in a strict legal sense which would either declare void *ab initio* any attempt to transfer the object, or give the heir a non-decaying right to reclaim the object itself. If all that inalienability in this literature means is that, say, land or a valued object retains the name of its original owner then that is a very thin notion of inalienability. In Icelandic law, as discussed on p. 103n8, there are rights of reclamation to ancestral land, but even these can be lost; see, e.g., *Grágás* Ib 79, II 411, where under certain conditions land-reclamation claims are subject to a limitations period. Consider, in the Bible, the restricted alienability of family land which is supposed to return to the lineage in the jubilee, *unless* it is a house in a walled city in which case there is only a one-year redemption period after which the transfer becomes irrevocable; Lev. 25:29. Nor is it always the case that the spirit of the object is not considerably stronger than the spirit of its original owner that supposedly suffuses it. Thus the practice of upwardly mobile noble families taking as their family name the name of the land they have come to occupy, whether acquired by plunder, gift, marriage, or inheritance; see, e.g., J.C. Holt, "What's in a Name? Family Nomenclature and the Norman Conquest," in his *Colonial England 1066–1215* (London, 1997), pp. 179–196. The object, or the land, thus ends up transforming the identity of the present possessor into the now dispossessed original giver. This is less a triumph of the spirit of the original owner, than that the thing that bears his name enables a kind of identity theft; I guess one might then say that so strong is the *hau* of the original owner that it transforms whoever comes into the property into that prior original owner in a sort of transmigration of souls. See further Graeber, *Toward an Anthropological Theory of Value*, pp. 193–215, esp. pp. 201–203, on potlatch and "name fastening" among the Kwaikiutl.

the gift of the bear by letting Audun travel to Svein, and Svein gives the ring to Harald via Audun and is thus both in on and in the gift. But we can see the special circumstances in *Audun's Story* that allow for that, for Harald is in a meaningful sense giving the bear to Svein, as Svein is truly repaying him for it with the ring, with Audun in each case acting as their agent.

Isleif is explicit about the value of the gift going up when Olaf gets in on the gift: "My lord, I thought this gift a splendid one when Brand gave it to me, but it has even greater value coming from you with these words." Isleif's words are sheer flattery. A future saint—Olaf—is prophesying about the spiritual gifts of a young priest, such that the king almost bows before him. That Brand must suffer his gift rating second place is the price Brand pays by having walked out of a story bearing his name and into the story of Isleif, future first bishop of Iceland.

Everything works out well here, because Olaf does not go through the motions of asking Isleif to hand back the cloak to him so that he can physically hand it over to Isleif. His reclamation and regiving are done verbally, almost virtually, as we would say nowadays. Brand thus gets to feel that his gift is not so much undone, as confirmed, despite Olaf compensating him and purporting to buy him out. Imagine though the round of hurt feelings and offense if Olaf dispossessed Isleif, failed to compensate Brand, and gave it to another person or kept it and handed it back to Isleif in an elaborate ceremony the next day.

There is still room for wondering what obligations exist after this tale. Who owes what to whom? Olaf has specified what he wants from Isleif: his prayers and intercession. He is buying protection or, less tendentiously, intercessory services. Surely Brand is owed by Olaf for having pointed out the optimal recipient of the cloak. How very much like the talent Audun had for finding perfect placements for debts. And Audun was repaid for his skill. That might be part of the reason Olaf compensates Brand for the cloak. He deserves something for discovering its highest and best use. This cloak has a biography[18] that, no matter how it is told, includes Brand centrally. His spirit imbues the gift, not

[18] On the biography of things see the classic treatments of Arjun Appadurai, "Introduction: Commodities and the Politics of Value," in Appadurai, ed., *The Social Life of Things: Commodities in Cultural Perspective* (Cambridge, 1986), pp. 3–63 and Igor Kopytoff, "The Cultural Biography of Things: Commoditization as Process," in Appadurai, ed., pp. 64–94.

quite in the same way Olaf's does, but it is there nonetheless; it would thus seem Isleif is not off the hook: he still is indebted to Brand.

A lot of valuable things can be regiven without insult or without any sense that propriety has been breached. When a certain Jon gives a valuable book, a *görsemi*, to the priest Gudmund, it is mentioned that it was the book that Bishop Pal had given Jon, but there is no sense that Jon has done Bishop Pal a wrong by giving his gift away. The new recipient, Gudmund, as Isleif was, is an appropriate one, who will become a bishop in due course also, and that more than satisfies the respect Jon owes the book and Bishop Pal who gave it to him.[19] And this adds yet another component to a gift's value. Its value is not just a matter of the soul of the giver that imbues it, but also the moral qualities and social standing of the person who receives it. That Svein accepts the bear raises its value, no differently than Isleif honors the coat by being the exact right person to wear it.[20] In fact, there is no story unless Audun's bear gets given to a person of account, a person already sagaworthy in his own right.

Giving away something given to you is capable of carrying exactly contrary meanings and a whole range of meanings in-between, depending

[19] *Guðmundar saga Arasonar*, ch. 34; see also Egil's regifting of King Æthelstan's gift to his friend Arinbjorn which Arinbjorn then repays by giving a sword to Egil that Arinbjorn had been given by Egil's brother; *Egils saga*, ch. 62. There is no suggestion of untowardness. Quite the contrary. The gifts are clearly meant to do honor to the recipients because of the fame of their prior possessors and, in any event, both gifts had been possessed for a number of years before having been passed on. Compare, however, Hallfred's compensation to Gris for having composed insulting verses about him. He pays over an arm ring, *Sigvaldanaut*, he received from Jarl Sigvaldi, but Hallfred had just received news of his lord's, Olaf Tryggvason's, death in battle in which Olaf was betrayed by Sigvaldi. The gift no longer has the value to Hallfred it once had (*Hallfreðar saga*, ch. 10). Gifts acquired by kings become part of their stock of wherewithal they constantly must draw on to reward retainers; recall that the axe Harald gave Halli was a gift to Harald (p. 38; and see below p. 118n7). One is clearly meant to take good care of gifts from honored givers; thus the words of a certain Bjorn who expresses reluctance to entrust to a fellow Icelander in Norway, whose integrity he has good reason to doubt, a gold ring Jarl Eirik gave him so that it can be taken to his betrothed back in Iceland : "it would be said I kept a weak grip on the jarl's gift if I let the ring pass into your hands"; *Bjarnar saga Hítdœlakappa*, ch. 3 (ÍF 3); see also *Laxdæla saga*, ch. 46 (sword and headdress).

[20] Parry, "*The Gift*, the Indian Gift, and the 'Indian Gift'," p. 468, remarks that the spiritual worth of the gift in Hinduism and Buddhism, in contrast to the orthodox Melanesian story of the giver's spirit providing the main source of value, depends on the quality of the recipient. This is also true in certain understandings of almsgiving in Christianity. The poor have a certain magical power to enhance the spiritual quality of transfers made to them.

on who is involved, the amount of time that has passed, the intentions of the giver and much more. Brand gives the cloak to Isleif not because he undervalues King Olaf or the cloak but because he so values both that he cannot think of anything more appropriate to honor the worthy Isleif.[21] Yet, as we well know, giving things away, especially things given to us as gifts, often means unloading objects which we have ceased to value very much. And there is anxiety on that score.

For a recipient to believe you really value the gift you are giving, it may be that the object must be of unassailably clear value (and could be cashed out for it), or (if there is no ready market for the thing) that it must hurt you to give it and that the pain is hard to disguise beneath the smiles and joy of handing it over.[22] And that joy need not even be entirely feigned, though it may be mixed with regret, for rituals of giving have a way of getting the actors to generate the appropriate sentiments to make the transactions succeed. We don't always have to fake our generous deeds.

The distrust of a gift's value by the recipient leads to some interestingly perverse behaviors.[23] Patrick Geary, in his writings on the relic trade, shows that it was thus better to claim that a relic a church acquired was stolen rather than received as a gift—though one then had to account for what kind of relic would be so weak as to have gotten stolen, unless it connived in its own theft to get owned by better clerics.[24] Who, after all, would give away a real miracle-working relic, unless it was losing its efficacy? Stealing it proved the thief valued it, and proved also that its proper owner did not disvalue it enough to give it away.

Return now to Audun giving to Harald the gift Svein gave to him and compare how differently it operates from Olaf's regiving the gift

---

[21] Compare Egil, old and blind and somewhat demented, who cannot tolerate the idea of the silver King Æthelstan had given him passing to heirs for whom his feelings are ambivalent at best. He prefers to sink it all in a hot spring before he dies. He also manages to kill the two slaves whom he ordered to guide him there; neither the silver nor the slaves, says the saga, were ever found; *Egils saga*, ch. 88.

[22] See my discussion in *Faking It* (Cambridge, 2003), ch. 7, regarding the easy fakeability of remorse. To see that an apology really hurts the apologizer to make it is one of the few ways we will accept it as being sincere, even though we suspect the person is only sorry for the pain it is causing him, not the pain he caused us.

[23] The deep distrust that pervaded buy/sell transactions, that one was being sold shoddy goods if the buyer, or could have gotten more for the object if the seller, is not completely avoided in the world of gifts.

[24] Patrick Geary, "Sacred Commodities: The Circulation of Medieval Relics," in Appadurai, ed., *The Social Life of Things*, pp. 169–191, at p. 186.

Brand gave. In the latter, there is a weak undoing and a redoing, two successive acts of giving the same object. In the former, there is one giving which simultaneously works as a complete gift from Svein and a complete gift from Audun, because Audun managed it so perfectly, by linking and merging the game he is playing with the kings to the game they are playing with each other. Olaf's way is clumsier, less grand, and makes one feel that it might well be accompanied with an almost childish chagrin of having lost the opportunity to maximize his gain from the gift by having given it away too soon to the wrong person.

GIFTS UPWARD: REPAYING BY RECEIVING AND FUNNY MONEY

Taking back a gift given, or handing on a gift received, is one thing; what if the person you are giving to doesn't want it? Notice again Audun's answer to Harald's question as to how Svein repaid him:

> The king then asked, "Did you get the animal to King Svein?
> "Yes, sire," he said.
> "How did he repay you?"
> Audun said, *"First, he accepted it."*
> The king said, "I would have repaid you the same way."

Audun's answer nicely confirms Pierre Bourdieu's claim that the actors in these highly scripted and even predictable exchanges experience them as anything but as certain and predictable as they might look to an outside observer.[1]

The obligation to accept

Svein's accepting the gift was not automatic. It might have been highly probable, but as Bourdieu points out, the difference between certainty and high likelihood is the difference between a sense of complacency on the one hand, and of being a nervous wreck, of being filled with anxious anticipation and stage fright that you might blow your lines so as to trigger a refusal, on the other. Svein might have said, sorry, I have more white bears than I need; we kings get so many of them these days from you Icelanders. Or why would I want to accept a bear from the likes of you; it is from Aki that I wish to accept the bear (for I could then repay him less, or not at all, claiming the bear to be Aki's repayment to me for having raised him up to high office). Or thanks, I am taking it, now get out of here before I have you killed.

Both parties to the gift exchange are speaking lines, acting a part, but the script is not written in stone and admits a lot of adlibbing. Thus the Icelandic delight in telling stories about how giving to King

[1] Bourdieu, *Outline of a Theory of Practice*, pp. 5–10.

Harald—given his delight in playing with the rules—defies routinization. Even the most rigid cultural scripts get acted out by people of different competence. People blow their lines, sometimes from ineptitude, sometimes by conscious design, sometimes from a desire to resist the likely outcome, or out of desire to insert modest amounts of playfulness, threat, challenge, and irony into routine expectations, as Harald loves to do. Some may delight in shifting the game entirely to one of seeing how well the parties can recover from a wrench (spanner) purposely thrown into the works to test one's own aplomb as Audun does with his No's or to test another's poise and tact or capacity for embarrassment.

And there is not just one script. The ways of giving and receiving, no different from the three manuscripts the story is preserved in, might follow varying scripts, providing plausible alternative ways of going about the process while still maintaining propriety or exercising a prerogative. Thus it is that when King Svein accepts the bear and admits his gratefulness, Audun can breathe a sigh of relief.

Mauss says that along with the obligation to requite a gift, there is the obligation to receive, as well as one to give in the first place. Kings, though, are able to play by different rules, indeed *must* play by different ones. It behooves kings, no less than it still does women, to be able to resist the "obligation" to receive in order to keep themselves from being bamboozled into having to repay. The stakes are higher for them. Saying No, with practice, might in time come fairly easy both to kings and women, or, if not—using an idiom still current in the early twentieth century—both would be "ruined."

We see from Audun's response to Harald that kings had already manipulated the expectations attending the obligatoriness of receiving. If there were an obligation to receive a proffered gift it did not bind them as it might bind an equal, a friend, or a would-be friend. A king, Audun suggests, accepts a gift by grace. When he can take what you are offering as plunder, tribute, toll, or tax, to accept it as a gift is to give up on more than a few royal prerogatives; it is to show favor.

Lords and nobles were aware of the stakes in these kinds of transactions. They had to make sure people did not use expectations emanating from a norm of reciprocity, that all gifts demanded returns, to paint them into a corner. It was for lords to play with the difference between high likelihood and certainty to control givers of gifts.

And play they did. Consider first the great ambiguity and manipulability of what counts as the *first* gift, which by being first effects the status of a countergift as being just that—second, a payback—instead of counting as itself the first gift in a new cycle. It could be claimed that the other so-called first gift merely closed off an earlier cycle, that it was thus itself a repayment, or that it did not qualify as a gift worthy of triggering reciprocity in any event. Firstness is something that was fought for, argued about, and could be gamed.[2] Indeed the struggle to determine firstness is one of the fundamental problems that legal systems must address. Thus the need for statutes of limitations, for rules of prescription, rules of finality such as *res judicata*, all in their way principles designed to finalize starting points, or wipe obsolete starting points off the legal and conceptual map. The Icelandic laws regarding reclamation of gifts we discussed in the previous chapter (p. 102), for instance, assume that it is readily discernible when a gift is the first gift in a cycle, when it is the unrecompensed one, rather than a payback for a prior gift. The very ease which the laws assume away the issue of firstness is perhaps evidence that these transactions were indeed more loans than gifts, as we suggested above. Determining the first in any succession of obligations is fraught with difficulty, no less than in feud than in gift-giving. In both, it is a matter of "spin" and politicking to define which wrong or hostile deed gets credited or blamed with setting the train of hostile exchanges in motion. Even what appears to us and others as Audun's free initiatory gift could have been understood by Audun as repaying Svein for Svein's virtue and the admiration it prompted in Audun.

Another common move available for lords and kings to finesse being held hostage by gifts from underlings was to take advantage of the ambiguity between a contract and a gift. When Svein makes Aki his steward, that can be understood as a reward for past services, the pretense being that it is a gift, but also as something like wages, or even as a contract for future services, and hence again not quite a gift, though the language of gift is employed both when it looks to reward past actions and to oblige future behavior.[3] The lines that separated gifts from loans, from contracts, from wages, from advance payments,

---

[2] For an account of a lord refusing gifts from his villagers so that he could first give them a festive meal and thus begin the exchange cycle so as to control the meaning of what was requiting what, see Ludolf Kuchenbuch, "Porcus donativus: Language Use and Gifting in Seigniorial Records between the Eighth and the Twelfth Centuries," in Algazi et al., pp. 193–246, at pp. 226–227.

[3] See Stephen D. White, "Service for Fiefs and Fiefs for Service: The Politics of Reciprocity," in Algazi et al., pp. 63–98, for an extended discussion of both the for-

especially when the same diction of giving, receiving, and requital was necessary to all of them, were blurry.[4] This allowed for parties to think one kind of transaction was happening, and not even be self-deceived or deceived when it was, but then later find that that transaction was eminently reinterpretable as something much less favorable to one of the parties.[5] This did not mean there were not easy cases, or that parties to a transaction could not be explicit about the definition of the exchange. This is a loan, Audun, with an interest rate of ten percent, principle and interest due in six months. But consider how much ambiguity was consciously noted by playing with words: Audun can thus make "repay" or "give" mean its opposite, "take", "receive", or "accept", "How did Svein *repay* you?...First, he *accepted* it."[6]

Kings were of course always free to reward those who gave them gifts or provided them loyal service and it was a good idea for them to do so on occasion, though not within the expectations of the gift-game, but more, again, either by pre-agreed contract or by grace. Grace is a doctrine in part developed to free higher ups, like God, from the shackles of the norm of reciprocity; grace derives its peculiar force from opposing

---

ward- and backward-looking aspect of grants of fiefs, as they remained ambiguously situated between gift and contract, countergift and wages.

[4] See above p. 36 where the competing idioms of purchase and gift are playfully manipulated by Harald and Halli.

[5] Algazi, "Doing Things with Gifts," p. 15: "Forms of gifting were often honored in the breach; one could incorporate some features of gift exchange into a transaction organized according to very different principles, or even just allude to gifts in passing in order to give a transaction a specific tinge." Algazi is discussing exchanges in the late Middle Ages which surely allowed for a greater variety of legally recognized forms of exchange than the more primitive societies that provided the basis for the classical anthropological theories of gift exchange using evidence from Micronesia, New Guinea, New Zealand, and the Pacific Northwest. See my *Bloodtaking*, ch. 3, in which I discuss how bargaining in certain saga dealings was less devoted to pinning down the price term, than to trying to negotiate the formal categorization of the exchange, that is, whether it was to be considered a gift, a contractual payment, a sale, a loan, or even an open expropriation.

[6] See Calvert Watkins, "New Parameters in Historical Linguistics, Philology, and Culture History," *Language* 65 (1989), 783–799, at pp. 786–788, who discusses the idea of reciprocity implicit in Indo-European *nem, yielding Germanic *niman*, to take, and Greek *nemo*, to give, distribute. He notes too that English "to take" can possess antithetical directional senses. I can take *from* someone who gives the object to me as a gift, or I can take something *to* someone and present it to him. I add the example of Old Norse *fá*, which means both to grab, to take, to obtain, but also to give or deliver into another's hands. And my daughter, Eva, points out to me the synonymity of caregiver and caretaker. See also Alain Guéry, "Le roi dépensier: le don, la contrainte et l'origine du système financier de la monarchie française d'Ancien Régime," *Annales ESC* 39 (1984), 1241–1269, at pp. 1243–1244.

itself to ideas of obligation and even to morals and good deeds, being by definition, if not actually in practice, free and unmerited.

No wonder then that so many medieval tales, fictional and non, complain about the niggardliness of lords and kings who do not know how to repay gifts and service properly. Avarice is taken to be the sure mark of a bad lord, at least in the view of the multitude of disappointed seekers of largesse.[7] Jarl Neri, recall, of *Gift-Ref's Saga*, made it a firm practice not to accept gifts because he could not bear to repay them. Unlike the many lords who took and then took their good time to make a repayment if at all, Jarl Neri felt the grip of a norm of reciprocity exquisitely. That is why he would not accept gifts. The one time he agreed to accept a gift, he repaid it with a shield, and it so depressed him to see the gap on the wall in his hall where the shields hung that Ref, the recipient, felt sorry enough for him to return it. But as we saw, the jarl still felt the obligation to repay in some way, as long as he would not have to part with any material goods of his own. He had no compunction about fulfilling his obligation to repay Ref's ox by providing Ref with a plan to capture other people's possessions.

Harald says he too would have accepted the bear, matching Svein's move to a T, as if this were in doubt after we had seen him ask for the bear as a gift when he first met Audun. Why then does he repeat the obvious? We know he would have accepted the bear. He means, it seems, to make a small joke at his own expense, but the joke depends on there being a real risk that a king might not accept, or not accept in a way the giver desires.

Bourdieu is right that there is a big psychological difference between certainty and high probability. And these kings like to emphasize that difference, because it keeps them freer, keeps a certain arbitrariness available to them. Is not the prerogative of arbitrariness the necessary explanatory condition in the first story (in the timeline of the Abra-

---

[7] See again White, "Service for Fiefs and Fiefs for Service," who discusses the problems lords had meeting the expectations of their followers for gifts of fiefs in 11th- and 12th-century French settings. Lords were always looking for ways to reclaim fiefs given, claiming breaches of obligation, or trying to prevent the fief from descending to the heir of an earlier donee, so that they could meet the impatient present expectations for reward of other men in their retinues. Lords were often aided by medieval mortality rates so that fiefs granted to vassals would not stay alienated for long before the lord's reversion became possessory. But deviations from the average in which one's prior grantees disappointed by not dying at predicted rates were common enough to cause lords no end of problems. See also Bartlett, *England under the Norman and Angevin Kings*, pp. 28–35.

hamic religions) ever told about a lord refusing to accept a gift? Cain thought so:

> In the course of time Cain brought to the Lord an offering of the fruit of the ground, and Abel brought of the firstlings of his flock and of their fat portions. And the Lord had regard for Abel and his offering, but for Cain and his offering he had no regard. So Cain was very angry, and his countenance fell. (Gen. 4:3–5)

There is thus more than a hint that when Audun says Svein *repaid* him by accepting the bear, that he is sincere, and that to his mind, at that moment at least, he was making a free gift. Acceptance, at a minimum, meant Svein had agreed not to foreclose the *possibility* of greater returns as he surely could have done had he resorted to the not infrequent royal tactic of forced sale at a low price or expropriation.[8] That within nanoseconds Audun could now figure that Svein bound himself to some form of positive reciprocity does not undo the freeness of the gift at the moment it was made.

But were he simply out to make a killing, Audun's worries could hardly have ended there. The rest of the colloquy reveals how much uncertainty Audun still must suffer. Part of the significance of the dialogue with Harald is to show how unspecific the repayment terms were in this case, with Harald himself having to check with Svein to get a sense of what would be fitting. If most gifts to kings had pretty standard values—gifts of horses, swords, jewels, axes, ships—that was not the case with polar bears.[9] The polar bear market was a thin one. Where does one look for the price term for something that rare? Yes, one might get kings to engage in a bidding war to help establish it, but in this case most of the bidding was hypothetical and ex post facto. Still, much of the strategizing in the gift game came in the form of

---

[8] That the same utterance could invite equally plausible contrary interpretations—that the gift of the bear was 'free' because the accepting of it was sufficient repayment, and that by accepting it Svein agreed to be bound to make further repayment—is testimony to how malleable the boundaries are between the various ways of styling gifts; sacrifices shade into obligatory gifts shade into free gifts, and can be in some circumstances now one now the other.

[9] In C.A. Gregory's model, one of defining characteristics distinguishing a gift from a sale is that the return for a gift is left open; it is unspecified; *Gifts and Commodities* (London, 1982). But that overstates the difference: there were pretty clear norms regarding what should requite what in most circumstances that greatly limited just how unspecified the form or value of the countergift could be. In fact, in many ritualized exchanges the return was specified in advance and this seems to be true across a wide variety of cultures. Not so, obviously, polar bears.

setting values for things that had no certain value, of determining an "equivalent." There were ranges of predictability, but they were ranges and probabilities, not certainties.

Giving up and down hierarchies: of God(s), beggars, and equals

I want to draw together observations the story makes about what it means to give to kings and to God. Consider this rough typology: 1) You can give to somebody not even in the game, as when the gift can be appropriately classified as alms to the wretchedly poor. 2) You can give to someone clearly beneath you in the social hierarchy who, unlike the poor, are still considered to occupy a respectable if lower social niche. A gift to them should bear no charitable associations; it is an honor to receive from a king or your lord, whether you are vassal or yeoman or Audun. 3) You can give to a rough equal, those, that is, you are openly competing with for honor. And 4) as we have seen in this story you can give upward, to a king, or to God or his agents, as when Audun goes to Rome.

The expectations of the actors, the possible moves and their meaning, the idea of what a gift is and does, the obligations it raises or does not raise, the probabilities of honor or insult, the harms or benefits it will confer, will vary considerably depending on the relative status of the players, and whether the context of the giving is religious or secular, openly competitive or with competitiveness obscured, formally ritualized or conventionalized more loosely. Not much inspection will show that the rough typology just presented has very porous boundaries separating one type from the other.

An obvious example of the classificatory difficulties: alms, for instance, gifts as far downward as you can go, can also count, depending on the precise theory being invoked, as gifts to God, as far up as you can go. So when Svein feeds and clothes Audun, a sick and destitute pilgrim, he is giving to a rather different Audun than the one who gave him the bear, and the gift is not to be understood properly as a payback for the bear. When Audun suggests to Harald that it was to be so classified, Harald subtly corrects him: "It's no great deal to do well by beggars; I would have done so too."[10] The poor have their role in theodicy, though

[10] Consider the difference between charity to the poor and liberality or largesse, which would describe gifts of a higher order, land, ships, office, to a different class of

it would make Kant blush to hear the reason the poor make for the best of all possible worlds. God, says one saint's life, created the poor as a gift to the rich, not as resources for cheap labor, but as a means to a rich man's salvation: "God could have made all mankind rich, but in fact He wanted there to be the poor in this world so that the rich would have by that means a way of redeeming their sins."[11] Gifts to the poor, in other words, are rather complex as to just who is properly playing the role of recipient and who the giver. And, as we shall see, gods and beggars share more than a few ways of paying back at something less than full value, if they are required to pay back at all.

Is, in fact, the beggar supposed to pay the almsgiver back? We saw that he is obliged to do so in Iceland should his fortunes improve. But that kind of repayment was a fond hope. Mostly a beggar discharged his duty as a recipient by merely accepting. He is not even understood to be bound to have to pray for the soul of his benefactor beyond a "God-bless" as a form of thanks. The rich man who scattered coins or sent his servants to hand out leftovers at the door was not about to bargain for prayers from such souls, as King Olaf bargained for prayers from the now poor but self-evidently on-the-rise holy man Isleif, and as many a benefactor of monks did by written agreement, but gifts to holy men already possessing socially recognized spiritual capital were not alms in the way alms to beggars were alms.

For the beggar, some small show of gratitude on his part would suffice, and even then the rich man might well find the poor so beneath contempt as not to care or bother to notice whether they were sincerely grateful or not. The demand for some show of gratitude varies in form depending on the particular circumstances of the gift, on the various styles of almsgiving.[12] The poor have fairly conventional thankings for

---

people; see Guéry, "Le roi dépensier," pp. 1245–1248, discussing 14th–16th century French matter.

[11] "Potuit nempe Deus omnes homines divites facere, sed pauperes ideo in hoc mundo esse voluit, ut divites haberent quomodo peccata sua redimerent," *Vita S. Eligii, Life of Saint Eloi* in J.-P. Migne, *Patrologia Latina* vol. 87, col. 533C (7th century), cited in Eliana Magnani S.-Christen, "Transforming Things and Persons: The Gift *pro anima* in the Eleventh and Twelfth Centuries," p. 272, in Algazi et al., pp. 269–284.

[12] The types of displays of gratitude vary widely across cultures. It is often remarked that in tribal or gift-exchange cultures gifts are not infrequently accepted without a word. Why express gratitude for a burdensome obligation that has just been imposed upon you? Says Van Wees, "Reciprocity in Anthropological Theory," p. 26: "our verbal displays of gratitude, it would seem, are shallow substitutes for a deeper sense of obligation and greater concern to reciprocate which characterizes other cultures." I am not sure that our sense of obligation is that much less intense. Western scholars

face-to-face handouts from the almsgiver that might take the form of groveling or proclaiming the greatness of the benefactor. Jesus loathed such spectacles and counseled giving alms in secret, but that only increases the burden on the recipient to appear sincere in this closer encounter in secret at the side door, whereas in public acts of benefaction the poor were more focused on jostling and pushing aside other poor to get to the scattered alms.[13]

Must God, or a king, act gratefully for the sacrifices, gifts, and prayers honoring him that come his way? Or will some small show suffice? Svein expressed gratitude to Audun when he received the bear: "To you, Audun, I owe such gratitude as if you had given me the whole animal." But in that case some clarifying statement was called for because Audun had said that the gift had been ruined by Aki, and that concern needed to be addressed. Moreover, this was no routine gift, but one that came with a tale attached to it of Audun's dedication and bravery in delivering it. Even a king could not help expressing gratitude, sincere gratitude.

But kings and God can accept without much more than a look of acceptance, a nod of the head in the case of a king, or the rise of the smoke of the sacrifice heavenward in the case of God. And kings and gods can get away with mere acceptance counting as a sufficient response because by accepting they have waived their right to say No, or zap the offeror for presuming to offer, even though he is obliged to offer. Rejecting offerings is something God (kings somewhat less) jealously reserved the right to do, as we saw in the case of Cain.

Pious commentators were desperate to expand upon the Genesis account of the Lord's rejection of Cain's offering. Genesis itself studiously refuses to reveal the actors' motives. Could the Lord be merely capricious in his favoritism? To save Him from no motives or bad ones, the commentators imputed good motives to Abel and bad ones

are too prone to find shallowness in western practice and confer depth on the primitive Other. The oppressiveness of the gift is alive and well among us. For those gifts for which thank-you notes are a conventional response, there is not much burden, unless you have recently tried to get one of your children to write them. In domains where something more is required than a routine note, we fully recognize the justness of Hobbes's observation (*Leviathan* I:11) quoted further below in the text.

[13] Some of whom might be tried as thieves if they tried to grab a share of an offering intended not for the poor, but for the monks and their saint; see R.C. van Caenegem, *English Lawsuits*, vol. 1, No. 14, p. 36.

to Cain.[14] And thereby the Lord is justified turning Abel into Audun (both deal in sheep), and Cain into Aki (both should be killed but get exiled instead).

What appears as arbitrariness to a disappointed seeker of favor is often suspected to be a deep and inscrutable policy of the king or god that puts people to desperate efforts to find the interpretive key to its method. Inscrutability was often cultivated by successful kings to keep people guessing. Thus Harald Finehair: "the king said little, as he was wont to do whenever he heard news of considerable importance."[15] The Norse evidence adduced so far suggests that it behooves God as well as kings to engage in strategic arbitrariness when it comes to accepting offerings and gifts. Arbitrariness in this domain becomes almost a privilege of office, and a very useful privilege at that, as long as it is not overused. It is hard not to see the Lord taking care to establish precisely this privilege with the first offering made to him—Cain's offering precedes Abel's. Reject first, thus making all subsequent givers anxious and uncertain, and then they will hold themselves "repaid" by mere acceptance. It is unclear whether God, like the beggar, was bound by a norm of reciprocity, but if he were or was concerned that he might be, we find him minting funny money to discharge any obligation that might have been raised: he could even claim that accepting (taking) means reciprocating.

Still, what does acceptance mean? Especially when the acceptance is made on behalf of the intended recipient, whether God or king, by an intermediary official: a steward, an abbot, accepting as agents, but with some vague proprietary interest of their own that is also hovering about. These agents may be expected to give back a little more than merely to proclaim that the higher up they represent has accepted the offering.

---

[14] See the materials assembled in Louis Ginzburg, *The Legends of the Jews* (Baltimore, 1953), 5 vols, 5:136n12.

[15] *Egils saga*, ch. 12; see too Henry of Huntingdon's description of Henry I of England as "a man of the deepest dissimulation and inscrutability of mind," quoted in Bartlett, *England under the Norman and Angevin Kings*, p. 29, discussing the vagaries of royal favor. Particularly interesting are the variations in the grantings and denials of quarter by King Sverrir or the alternations of brutal reprisal and easy forgiveness of William the Conqueror. One can explain ex post why it was rational to make the particular move at the time, but no one could from an ex ante position be sure which Sverrir or William would show up, the lenient or the cruel one; nor could Sverrir or William predict which strategy would produce the desired result in any particular instance. Both must have felt that keeping others guessing was their best strategy over the long haul.

The agents might have to offer membership in a monastic community, good fortune, prayers, or sometimes even a pocketable quid pro quo.

There are other leakages in the boundaries separating God from the wretched beggar. Both God and the beggar—in the view of an uncharitable outsider, or even in the eyes of an insider despairing of God's grace—receive without paying back much if at all, and both seldom appear satisfied; they thus keep hitting you up, asking for more. Once you give, you're marked as a mark. This observation has long been noted with regard to medieval lordship. Beware of giving a gift to a lord or to a king once, for he might well insist on making it an annual event.[16] Gifts upward have a way of becoming regularized as taxes or tribute. Though gifts upward and tribute are not the same in cultural or social terms, an economist may be hard-pressed to find the difference between them (except as regards their attendant transaction costs); even some of their cultural and social meanings overlap.

Gifts between rough equals are clearly obligation-creating. Gifts can thus be burdensome; they can even humiliate the recipient if they are of such value that the recipient would be hard-pressed to make adequate recompense, because as between equals the return must be demonstrably of equivalent value; no funny money paybacks. There is, as *Audun's Story* shows regarding the equals Harald and Svein, an inherent, nearly unavoidable competitiveness that lurks in the shadows of the most friendly and routine of exchanges. This is standard fare not only in the literature on gift-exchange but also in proverbs and wisdom literature widely expressed across cultures. Hobbes minces no words:

> To have received from one, to whom we think our selves equall, greater benefits than there is hope to requite, disposeth to counterfeit love; but really secret hatred; and puts a man into the estate of a desperate debtor, that in declining the sight of his creditor, tacitely wishes him there, where he might never see him more. For benefits oblige; and obligation is thraldome; which is to ones equall, hateful (*Leviathan* I.11).

An Icelandic saga makes the point even more starkly: Egil and Einar were both poets. Egil was older and Einar learned much from frequent conversation with Egil about their art. When Einar returned from Norway he sought out Egil at his home. Egil was away so Einar departed

[16] Marc Bloch, Feudal Society, trans. L.A. Manyon (Chicago, 1964), p. 206; Alain Guéry, "Le roi dépensier" pp. 1256–1257; but see Kuchenbuch, "Porcus donativus," p. 230. A law of the Norwegian Gulaþing, (NGL I, p. 58) attributed to Magnus the Good (d. 1047), repeals the exaction of obligatory "Christmas gifts" to the king.

leaving behind for Egil a gift of a bejeweled shield that Einar had received from Jarl Hakon for a verse he had composed honoring the jarl. When Egil returned he asked what the shield was doing there. He was told it was a gift from Einar. Egil responded: "Damn the wretched bastard. Does he expect me to stay up all night and compose a poem on his shield? Get my horse; I am going to ride after him and kill him."[17] Luckily Einar had a head start and Egil could not overtake him; he calmed down and composed a poem.

It is just this kind of imposition, which generates the murderous response in Egil that is so much more muted in gifts upward and gifts clearly downward like alms. The reason should be clear. When the hierarchy is secure, as when an Audun gives to a Svein, the gift might still be a challenge to Svein to repay it in some way, but it is hardly a challenge in which Audun is competing for rank with the king he is giving to, or competing with him in a contest of generosity. Audun, if he is competing, is competing against other would-be givers to kings, or against other Icelanders trying to make a name for themselves abroad, while the king is competing reputationally against other kings, but those competitions are quite remote from the primary exchange between Audun and Svein. Aki can be sent away gnashing his teeth at Audun's fortune, Harald can be compelled to admire Svein, but as between Audun and Svein the gift is not charged with anywhere near the poison it bears as between equals.

Nadab and Abihu: sacrifice, caprice, and binding God and kings

Let me return to the matter of superiors cultivating some amount of arbitrariness as a strategy to avoid being locked in by gifts from inferiors. Again, the practice is always trickier and more complex in the range of possible behaviors than any rough set of rules can account for. If God's random refusal of Cain's offering made Cain murderous, consider that God too (not unlike Harald with Ulf the Wealthy) might play murderously with an occasional offeror. The tabernacle has just been finished; the high priests have been consecrated and the dedicatory offerings are being made. Aaron blesses the people and a fire comes from before

[17] *Egils saga*, ch. 81.

the Lord and consumes the burnt offering, indicating acceptance of the sacrifices. Then:

> Nadab and Abihu, the sons of Aaron, took either of them his censer, and put fire therein, and put incense thereon, and offered strange fire before the Lord, which he commanded them not. And there went out fire from the Lord, and devoured them, and they died before the Lord. (Lev. 10:1–2)

A few minutes earlier fire issued forth to consume the lambs and other offerings, which was taken as a beneficent sign of acceptance. It seems that either the Lord was in the mood to consume things and could not stop with mere lambs after the sweet aroma of the burnt offerings he had just accepted had whet his appetite or, more likely, given the harshness of his response, he meant to remind the congregation not to count on offerings being so easily accepted as his welcoming consumption of Aaron's offering had been.

The rabbinical commentators had no less trouble with this instance of divine caprice than they did with the Lord rejecting Cain's offering. Some decided Nadab and Abihu were drunk, though the biblical text indicates little more than that they, perhaps in an access of exuberance, were making an additional offering, a supererogatory offering, to further honor the Lord; a free gift, since it was not commanded. There is no evil intent mentioned; it seems mostly that their failure was the sin of improvisation.[18]

The Lord could hardly have been threatened by Nadab's and Abihu's desire to give him more fine aromas. There was no poison in their gift in the way Egil thought Einar's may have imposed a burdensome if not lethal obligation upon him. The Lord seems to be using the same strategies that we saw Harald employ so expertly. Do not let anyone come to think that acceptance (or repayment) is automatic, even if the giver has *proper* intentions. Reserve unto yourself the power of caprice. It may well be rational to do so, otherwise you might become too predictable, and thus manipulable by inferiors.[19]

---

[18] *Jewish Study Bible*, ed. Adele Berlin and Marc Zvi Brettler (Oxford, 2004), p. 227 n10:1–3.

[19] On low-status people manipulating the high and for a ritual meant to extract aid from the powerful consider the Indian custom of sitting dharna in which the claimant debases himself ostentatiously before a person to embarrass him into granting the requested relief; similar prostrations and beggings are frequently attested in various medieval sources; see, e.g., *Njáls saga*, ch. 88 (Hrappr); see generally Geoffrey

And you need not acquire either a reputation for injustice or avarice if you sin against the norm of reciprocity from time to time, for a few capricious acts, just like an occasional brutal one, will make people warier, and respectful. It will mean that no one will take for granted that you will either accept their gifts, or make a return if you accept: you want to make your acceptance an act of grace, not a fulfillment of a duty. You might even want your generosity to bear an aura of threat. William the Conqueror thus pretends to stab the palm of the abbot of La Trinité-du-Mont whose hand is extended to accept the knife that betokens formal delivery of the land. William accompanied the feint "jokingly" (*ioculariter*) with the line: "This is the way land ought to be given."[20] There is real wit here, with William playing ominously on the legal term of art of giving land "by means of the knife."[21] The knife is in William's joke both a symbol of the land being conveyed and a completely non-symbolic lethal weapon, which he then turns into a symbolic lethal weapon by making the thrust of it a feint. The tale captures perfectly how astute William was at unnerving the recipients of his largesse; he made sure their pleasure was adulterated with a good dose of fear, thus reminding them never to be complacent about his "obligation" to give, to receive, or to make the kind of return that would please them. William knows there is more than one way to lace a gift with poison.

But the risk of being constrained by the power of a never-quite-deniable norm of reciprocity was surely a risk for the Lord no less than for kings. What are petitionary prayers meant to do? Though they do not officially pretend to bind God to perform, they can hardly not be meant to constrain the pure freedom He claims by the doctrine of grace. Pope Gregory I said that the faithful could actually make God their debtor by giving to Him.[22] God, assumes Gregory, can be forced

---

Koziol, *Begging Pardon and Favor: Ritual and Political Order in Early Medieval France* (Ithaca, NY, 1992).

[20] *Regesta Regum Anglo-Normannorum: The Acta of William I (1066–1087)*, ed. David Bates (Oxford, 1998), No. 232, cited in Hudson, *Land, Law, and Lordship*, p. 163.

[21] For a similar style of dark humor taking a legal term of art and wittily recalling its brutal literalism, see Nahash's grim joke to the men of Jabesh-Gilead. Nahash plays off the Hebrew for "to make a covenant," which is literally "to *cut* covenant": "On this condition will I 'cut' it with you, that I may thrust out all your right eyes" (1 Sam. 11:2–3); see my discussion in *Eye for an Eye* (Cambridge, 2006), pp. 44–45.

[22] "Deum vobis fecistis procul dubio debitorem," in *S. Gregorii Magni Registrum epistularum* II, 25, ed. Dag Norberg (Turnholt, 1982), p. 111, cited in Bernhard Jussen,

to play by Odin's rule: "a gift always seeks its return."[23] No God, claiming omnipotence, or no gods claiming merely the godlike prerogative to be arbitrary and capricious, can let themselves be gamed like so many kings in *Gift-Ref's saga*. That, however, is just what so many of the faithful try to do.

But are gifts to God properly gifts? Sometimes they take the form of sacrifices, which may implicate different responses, different expectations. Though gifts and sacrifices share certain features, they are not completely congruent. Does any difference between them figure in *Audun's Story*? Audun's gift to Svein is very much a gift, even though he almost starves getting it to him, in a way his pilgrimage to Rome is not about gifts, though it too almost kills him.

Take three distinct deliveries that Audun engages in: payment to his kinsman Thorstein to fund his mother for three years of food and lodging; the gift of the bear to Svein; and the pilgrimage to Rome. The first is a support obligation demanded by law; though it involves a "sacrifice" on the part of Audun, it is a payment for services. The second is a gift; though it involves extraordinary risk of loss its point is not to lose, materially or otherwise.

The third, the pilgrimage, may indeed have some sacrificial aspects: thus his near death and suggested resurrection at Easter time, as he is bathed, washed, and taken back into the retinue. Yet even the pilgrimage holds out the prospect of gains, supposedly spiritual and mostly postponed to the future, though, in *Audun's Story*, some portion of these prospects are arguably transmuted into worldly rewards here and now. The pilgrimage was undertaken as a free act; and though it could also be

---

"Religious Discourses of the Gift in the Middle Ages: Semantic Evidences (Second to Twelfth Centuries)," in Algazi et al., pp. 173–192, at p. 176; see further the discussion on binding God with gifts in S.-Christen, "Transforming Things and Persons," p. 281: "The notion that by lending alms to God, man makes Him into his debtor had already been upheld by the Greek and Latin fathers, by John Chrysostom, Cyprian, or Ambrose."

[23] *Hávamál*, st. 145. Regarding saints: "The fact that while alive the saint received gifts was itself already a reason for requiring miracles from him in return. The principle of 'a gift ought to be rewarded' was one of the basic principles of social relations in barbarian and early feudal society and it also extended to relations between laymen and saints"; Aron Gurevich, *Medieval Popular Culture: Problems of Belief and Perception*, trans. János M. Bak and Paul A. Hollingsworth (Cambridge, 1988), p. 40. Gurevich was the first to apply anthropological understandings of gift exchange to Norse material; see "Wealth and Gift-Bestowal among the Ancient Scandinavians" *Scandinavica* 7 (1968), 126–138. On saints making sure they collected return gifts for the cures they effected see John H. Arnold, *Belief and Unbelief in Medieval Europe* (London, 2005), p. 87.

seen as a pious duty and hence not quite free, there is no enforcement mechanism to motivate the pilgrim to fulfill the duty except his own free will. But I do not wish to put too much stock in these distinctions. The lines separating a gift from a sacrifice, once we get dismemberment, blood, and slaughter out of it, get to be quite fuzzy.[24]

What then is the difference between gifts upward to a king and sacrifices upward to god or his agents? One attempt to define the difference, based on medieval Latin distinctions in terminology, is that *offerings*, which we might call sacrifices, are consistently responded to by being *accepted*. An offering is accepted; that's it and that's all: no reciprocation. Reciprocation is reserved for divine remuneration of good works; works trigger a payback obligation on God's part.[25] Noteworthy in this distinction is its desire to effect a compromise by carving out one area—offerings—in which a movement of goods upward gets classified as a sacrifice which leaves the deity free to accept or reject them but triggers no further repayment obligation, while conceding a space—good works—in which the deity agrees to play by the rules of reciprocity. This seems too neat to me—how, for instance, does one classify almsgiving, works or offering? And then consider that as

[24] See further below on the ideology of the free gift, pp. 135–138. Attempts have been made to adopt a less sanguinary understanding of sacrifice. Anthropologist, C.A. Gregory, distinguishes between gifts to men and gifts to God in that the latter are sacrificial in the sense that they involve a complete surrender of title to the recipient, a complete transfer of ownership; "Gifts to Men and Gifts to God: Gift Exchange and Capital Accumulation in Contemporary Papua," *Man* 15 (1980), 626–652, at p. 645. No spirit of the *hau* inheres in a gift to God, no parts of the giver's soul inhabit the object desperate to get it back to its true home with the giver. But the degree of alienation, whether total or conditional, does not provide an explanation for a difference between a gift and a sacrifice. It begs the question of why the gods are released from having to make a repayment. Others eliminate the deity's payback obligation by invoking a different understanding of the rights in the object given. Rather than giving over a full title to the deity, a title that was yours alone before the transaction, a sacrifice can be understood instead to be rendering what is Caesar's unto Caesar. God has a supervening lien in assets that may be yours as against another human being, but are not yours as against God. In the Bible when a person offers or sacrifices the first fruits or the first born he is not giving what is *his* to give, but giving *back* to God what is God's. It is God's *hau* that is being honored. I am not sure this works as an explanation that is not conclusory either: by a fiat of definition, it relieves the gods of being bound to reciprocate. On the divine lien in Talmudic property theory, see Madeline Kochen, *The Divine Lien*, forthcoming.

[25] Jussen, "Religious Discourses of the Gift," pp. 182–188: "A survey of the semantic field of *munus* reveals a limited range of notions about how a *munus* was transferred. It was 'offered' (*offerre*) and 'accepted' (*accipere*), 'regarded' or 'not regarded' (*respicere, non respicere*); only seldom was it simply 'given' (*dare*)" (p. 183).

a psychological matter the distinction is impossible to maintain, for if sacrifices are *accepted* again and again and they produce no palpable improvement in crops, fertility, luck, peace, or victory, then I would not be surprised to see people start to stint on their sacrifices or offerings, even punish their saints and gods, or shift their allegiance entirely.

Funny money that is not so funny

If one were to be cynical one might note that those very high in the relevant hierarchy, like kings and gods, when they do admit a payback obligation beyond mere acceptance, get to pay back with funny money. Not Svein; he pays over material goods of great marketable value, but he cannot reward all good gifts this way or he would soon be bankrupt. He must pick and choose. Harald, however, pays in funny money when he matches Svein with "would haves", which are something akin to God paying in the form of IOU's redeemable in an afterlife with no recourse should they turn out not to be honored.

But royal funny money often qualifies as symbolic capital to those who get paid in it and some symbolic capital can have a real price put on it and be cashed out for material goods or increase one's opportunities for acquiring real goods. Consider this case: an Icelander named Thorvard Crowbeak has his attempt to give King Harald a ship's sail refused by Harald, which Thorvard then gives to Harald's brother-in-law, Eystein. Eystein later repays the sail by giving Thorvard a cloak "because this cloak ranks as well against most other cloaks, as this sail ranks against most other sails." The next day Eystein comments further on the countergift he made to Thorvard: "It wasn't destined that the king accept your sail, but *I figure that had he accepted it he would have repaid it just as I have. But you have received nothing for the fact that it was not a king who repaid you.* I cannot help that I am not as high-ranking as a king. So accept this gold ring in consideration of the difference between the king's and my rank."[26]

Some kinds of funny money, it thus seems, are no joke: they have a cash value, but that cash value is not a cost the king must pay, so it is funny for him, but not for others. There is something like a market in kingly gifts and signs of favor, a market in which the king does not

[26] *Thorvard Crowbeak's Story* (*Þorvarðar þáttr krákunefs*, M ch. 41, ÍF 6:369–374).

participate except to furnish it with capital from which others take the profits. Eystein admits that Harald, had he accepted the sail, could properly discharge his repayment obligation with a countergift of less market value than Eystein can get away with, because the same gift from a king has more prestige. And in this story a precise price of one gold ring is put on the difference in prestige of getting a cloak from a king as opposed to getting it from a magnate, the king's brother-in-law. The king could thus get off more cheaply had he accepted the sail.

To an Audun, say, back home in the Icelandic system of valuation, the value of owning a sword and a cloak from King Harald could be realized in various ways without ever having to transfer them. For merely having received them, a class of women, for instance, from wealthy families or wealthy in their own right, would now be eligible as wives that were well above the league Audun was playing in before he set out on his adventure; his stock in every sense would go up for having received royal favor, and some of that favor could be cashed out.

But, Eystein notwithstanding, there was no system of pricing this prestige or symbolic capital with any precision in the gift-exchange world. Eystein is thus being consciously magnanimous in a wryly sagaworthy way (he is overpricing the difference in value, if anything), by reducing to exactitude a value that is meant to be fuzzy and loose. The difference in value of a cloak coming from Eystein rather than Harald is not priceable in the way flour sold in a market is (or even a wardship or a marriage might be): the wit of *Thorvard Crowbeak's Story* depends on that, similar to the way that much of the narrative force of *Audun's Story* depends on the indeterminacy of pricing a polar bear with a special story attached to it.[27] The evaluation of prestige had too much play in the joints, too many variables for there ever to be in Bourdieu's sense a "perfect interconvertibility" between symbolic capital and cash.[28]

Eystein also points to another matter worth attending to: kings and nobles in these stories, above all in *Audun's Story*, do not cringe, as would many an academic, at the idea of trade and markets. There is a fairly

---

[27] Wergeld systems show that precise monetary differences between juridical ranks could be scheduled formally in laws, but the precision of wergeld schedules was itself often a kind of spurious precision when it came to settling actual disputes. Nonetheless, wergeld starts with an assumption of precision which makes more sense in the more exacting legal mode than it would in the game of gift exchange which depends on there being considerable discretion and unpredictability in value determination.

[28] See p. 51n4.

easy mingling of gift-exchange and the market as when we see kings giving gifts of trading vessels loaded with trade goods and a bag of silver along with gifts clearly meant to operate in a prestige system of valuation, like a cloak, a sword, an arm-ring. The gifts of merchandise and hacked silver or coins were meant to be exchanged for a profit in market transactions and yet were still gifts meant to honor their recipient by paying him in a medium that had nothing funny about it, as certain prestige gifts might.[29]

It has been claimed of late that the norm of reciprocity, Odin's law, is something of a sham. It is said to be too manipulable by the powerful, who often paid back in funny money for real goods received, and it is often used too loosely by academics who succeed in making it nearly as vacuous as the self-interest tautology is. With a little imagination, something can always be found to be a return for something else.[30] You give the king a polar bear and he "gives back" his acceptance, his waiver of his right to refuse. But I want to reaffirm in the face of various revisionisms that claim that the norm of reciprocity is meaningless as an explanatory principle of social action, or more nefariously, that it is nothing more than ideological persiflage that obscures the expropriation of the oppressed by an oppressor, that the norm is still alive, well, and meaningful. Even God and kings cannot whisk the norm away; they feel constrained to pay some homage to it, though that homage

[29] This is not to say that merchants and traders could not be sneered at, if they were not also clearly warriors or long-distance traders. Local peddlers, for instance, were standardly objects of scorn in the sagas.

[30] See, e.g., Parry, "*The Gift*, the Indian Gift, and the 'Indian Gift'," p. 466, critiquing recourse to the norm of reciprocity as an explanation for social action, especially in gift exchange. More recently, Graeber criticizes the looseness of the term "reciprocity," which "as currently used...is very close to meaningless"; *Toward an Anthropological Theory of Value*, p. 217. The obligations to give, to receive, to repay, he says, are felt with varying force or with no force at all depending on the practice and the culture. As I say in the text, the ingenuity of any researcher or any clever operator playing the exchange game can find something reciprocating something else, even if it be as absurd as the notion that the fist that hits the face is being met as hard by the face. But that anthropologists and historians should start worrying about the analytical robustness of the norm of reciprocity given that the people they are studying were always grumbling about inadequate repayment or making jokes about getting stiffed, is less because scholars tend to be blind to wit, as because the contentlessness of the norm claimed by those attacking it is overstated. Still, it is true that the notion of reciprocity has been deployed in rather different ways depending on the researcher. See the discussion in van Wees, "Reciprocity in Anthropological Theory." See also Marshall Sahlins's influential schema in *Stone Age Economics* (Chicago, 1972), ch. 5. Among medieval historians, see the essays in Algazi, et al., especially Algazi's "Doing Things with Gifts."

be paid at times in false or debased coin, or at a substantial discount rate, or not as regularly as one would like. Nonetheless, it is true that certain mystifications work in their favor when it comes to pricing the value of their returns that are not readily employable by equals when dealing with each other. God, kings, and lords get easy forgiveness of their gift debts, so that if they let five gifts go unrequited they can, by requiting the sixth, be gratefully understood to have repaid all outstanding repayment obligations, similar to the way a few acts of mercy capriciously sprinkled here and there could generate enough good will to enable an extended course of oppressive "justice" and thus get even the irascible and jealous Yahweh called merciful.

The norm of reciprocity also was understood to encompass gifts of negative value, to matters, that is, of justice and revenge. The Icelanders saw, indeed the golden rule itself sees, gifts of positive and negative value as being on a single reciprocity axis. If someone did you a good turn, you would be shamed if you did not return the favor and, likewise, if someone did you a bad turn you would be shamed if you did not pay it back. Both good and evil demanded reciprocation. Says one Icelandic mother to her husband and sons about the scurrilous verses she has just heard had been composed about them: "*Gifts* have been given to you, father and sons alike; and you would scarcely be men if you did not repay them."[31] Our idiom "to give as good as you get" shows we still participate in that conceptual world.[32] Feud and revenge itself were a subset of the world of gift-exchange. And on the negative as well as on the positive side paybacks came in different amounts, sometimes at

[31] *Njáls saga*, ch. 44, trans. Magnusson and Pálsson (Harmondworth, 1960). Women were significant players in the exchange of "gifts" of negative value, exchanging devastating insults, but were less visible as players in the positive gift-exchange system and then mostly as queens, one particular queen in especial: Gunnhild, wife of Eirik Bloodaxe. But in homelier Iceland women could give slaves freedom and fund them, or assist outlaws by providing them hospitality, or give hay and food to a neighbor who has run short. The grand matriarch Unn the Deep-Minded could make gifts of granddaughters in marriage, or gifts of land (*Laxdæla saga*, chs 4–7), but this is rather different than classical competitive gift exchange.

[32] The Icelandic mother's and our own idiom tracks more closely Gouldner's idea of negative reciprocity as revenge than Sahlin's notion of negative reciprocity which lumps feuding raids together with market exchange; Alvin W Gouldner, "The Norm of Reciprocity: A Preliminary Statement," *American Sociological Review* 25 (1960), 161–178, at p. 172. Feud and commercial exchange are rather obviously different, academic marxisant commitments notwithstanding. At the very least in market exchanges the pretense is often maintained of doing someone a good turn, or certainly not doing them a bad one; not so feud; see van Wees, "Reciprocity in Anthropological Theory," p. 24.

ten cents on the dollar, but some amount of requiting was expected or you were no man, a god maybe, but not a man worth attending to any longer, unless you were sure enough of your ability to retaliate so as to give forgiveness as an occasional gift.[33]

A good god though must make sure there is rain for the crops, so if it rains he can be credited with making a return for all the offerings he has received. The god still might insist the rain is by grace, but that is not how the recipients of it will wholly see it; for them it is god yielding a return. A good king gets credit for rain too (and blame for drought), just as today presidents or prime ministers get praised or blamed for economic prosperity or recession for which their inputs have negligible effect, if any at all. *Audun's Story* even casts its clever eye in this direction when Audun gives all the credit for his good luck to Harald. Was the king getting more credit than he deserved? There is no false consciousness or self-deception when Audun so credits him. But that does not quite resolve the funny money problem. Harald deservedly gets his credit, true, but mostly because he took great care to cultivate a reputation that led everyone dealing with him to expect the worst. Harald manages to make sentiments of gratitude nearly congruent with feelings of relief. By simply not being cruel—the benchmark expectation when dealing with him—he is credited with kindness. So he gets credit for repaying a debt by not being as bad or as cheap as he could have been. Thus has he minted a special coinage—absence of rapaciousness and cruelty—that keeps his repayments rather nicely affordable.

---

[33] Negative gifts of insult and harms did not play completely by the same rules as positive gifts. Only a hot-headed fool paid back every wrong done him. One picked and chose when to make a return. As I have written before: the wise bloodfeuder made sure that others believed that he would avenge the *next* wrong done him, though he ignored the present one.

OF FREE AND CLOSING GIFTS

We granted earlier that at the moment Audun gave Svein his bear, he gave it freely. The gift was free, but only for nanoseconds before it started to change its hue.[1] The free gift is the gift that transcends the force of the norm of reciprocity and hence escapes the trammels and temptations of self-interest, for freeness means not only that the gift need not have been made in the first place, but that once made and accepted it raises no obligation, moral or otherwise, to make a return. It is thus free at the front and back end: it is not obligatorily given, nor once given does it oblige a return.

The free gift is conceptually and even psychologically parasitical on Odin's rule. It is a reaction to it. The norm of reciprocity comes first. This is why the free gift has to be asserted by fiat: it must be called into being by something with the power to override the default rule, the rule of reciprocity, which seems to be hardwired into us. The pre-Socratics made reciprocity a principle of cosmic symmetry. Summer was understood to pay back winter; then winter returned the favor, each giving as good as it got, because any form of giving, whether positive or negative, demanded giving back.[2]

The idea of the free gift is part of a set of doctrines that maintains certain hierarchies. Who is it that gets to rise above or sink below Odin's insistence on equivalence? Who can claim that they do not have to return a favor? Or that favors they grant cannot be repaid even if the recipient tries to repay them so as not to feel himself indebted and perpetually burdened? It is God and gods, kings and lords, who give and take by grace or whim. And when the low give "freely" to those above them, it is understood to be less a gift than a sacrifice, which the gods either accept or reject and that ends the matter. With sacrifice (taxes, offerings, tribute), subservience is confirmed and often imposed by authoritative force. The free gift upward was often felt as a burden,

---

[1] See above p. 119.

[2] See Gregory Vlastos, "Equality and Justice in Early Greek Cosmologies," *Classical Philology* 42 (1947), 156–178. It is in Anaximander that winter is seen as paying back summer for its hot aggression.

an unwelcome duty,[3] so that one required a gift of grace to be able to achieve the psychological state to be able to give freely. In some settings free comes to mean its opposite as when a gratuity is simply part of the bill to be paid.[4]

The doctrines that announce the free gift often take on a kind of insistence, imposed either by theological dogma or by positive law. By the 19th century the Anglo-American law had declared that what makes a gift a gift and not a contract or loan is that it is free, even, or especially, as between rough equals.[5] If the giver reneges on promises that he was going to make a gift the would-be donee has no cause of action at law to compel the transfer. And if the giver actually handed it over, he had no action for its recovery if the donee were an ingrate and did not repay the now free gift with love and affection, honor and obedience, or a more concrete return gift.[6]

How very different from medieval Icelandic and Norwegian law, where a gift that did not elicit a return gift gave rise to a cause of action. Except in one telling instance where the law's fiat makes a gift free whatever the intention of the "giver" may have been, and, not surprisingly, it is a gift upward: thus a person who has his household on a church farm is required to maintain the buildings and walls, but if he "improves church land, then he shall have God's gratitude for it. He cannot claim money as compensation for it."[7] God's gratitude (*Guðs þakk*)" contains a kind of smirk in it for the improver being such a fool: the phrase in this setting becomes a synonym for "sorry, tough luck," not a statement of God's obligation to say thank you.

There is an economics that sustains the doctrine of the free gift. It requires abundance or plenitude. God's grace is infinite and can

[3] A duty by itself need not offend the idea of freeness. Duties can surely be discharged willingly, even with a certain joyfulness. And for those that need a bit more effort to discharge one can cultivate the virtue of dutifulness, which need not carry a grim Puritanism with it.

[4] See also p. 129n24. It is frequently observed, but still worth noting here, how the words for tax bore all the ironies that arise from euphemism: duty, custom, gratuity, or in medieval to Ancien Regime France, *don*, gift.

[5] Likewise the German law code, effective as of 1900, in which gifts are defined as free; see discussion in Wagner-Hasel, "Egoistic Exchange and Altruistic Gift," p. 150.

[6] There is a small exception carved out in some cases for returns of engagement rings when the engagement is broken off. Though the gift met all the requirements of a completed gift at the time of transfer, it was deemed in fact to be conditional on getting married; see, e.g., among a number of cases, Heiman v. Parrish, 262 Kan. 926, 1997.

[7] *Grágás* Ib 217, II 59–60.

therefore be generated at no cost to himself; that is perhaps why the common law did not come around to defining a gift as free until England and America were the richest countries on earth, when, in other words, free gifts were not so costly to make. But then freeness seems not always to be as free as declared, or not always a blessing when free, even amidst plenty. Freeness not only requires abundance, it requires aggressive monitoring to keep Odin's norm of reciprocity from sneaking back in to attach strings to the gift. Free gifts are meant to elicit gratitude, praise, and obedience if given by the high to the low, or bring good fortune and protection, if delivered by the low to the high, as we touched on before.

A further word on gratitude: Gratitude may be understood to be a subset of a larger category of propitiary sentiments, behaviors, and rituals. If the free gift is from high to low it must elicit instant and insistent displays of thankfulness to ward off the wrath of the giver. Free gifts from the low to the high, from worshiper to the gods, are often openly propitiary, taking the form of thanking or praising the deity for his lovingkindness, or giving him his blood upfront, so as to ward off his ready wrath. Gratitude is intimately bound up with love, even a form of it, but it is also bound up with fear. Thus the near synonymity of "fear of the Lord" and "love of the Lord".

But it is not only the Lord or the gods who demand what are claimed to be free gifts. The deities are more than matched by the demandingness of the lowly worshiper. The selfless love that can inform all-consuming worshipful gratitude once mixed with the theological virtue of hope—the function of which was to keep one's faith from crumbling in the face of the one's own and the world's suffering—begins to engender optimistic expectations, which then crystallize into what are powerfully felt as rightful claims on the deity to make good on what one hoped for. God is then held to account.

Add a new wrinkle, one that works, at least on its face, more in favor of the low than the high. The ethnographic literature suggests offerings to God may be rather more toxic than the usual poison in the gift, which is generally understood to be a metaphor for the obligation to repay and the competition for honor that attends the exchanges. Suppose, however, that the gift has negative value to the giver, that to his mind if he retains it he will be poisoned. He thus gives over to (or loads upon) the deity his sins, his troubles, his bad luck, his junk, and sometimes even claims tax deductions for it. In various Hindu traditions, for instance, lower-caste gifts upward to Brahmins are explicitly toxic, emblems of bad fortune.[8] The recipient of such poisoned gifts is, as far as the giver is concerned, a scapegoat whose job is to bear unpleasant things off to the wilderness never to be seen again. Consider in this light Jesus the Lamb who—in accordance with the rules requiring the sacrificial victim to be without defect—is in a state of ritual purity and is also the freest of gifts because self-given by his own grace. But this pure Lamb is weighed down with the poison of all our sins, a scapegoat, sacrificed to propitiate a Father who insists on being paid back for man's first disobedience. There is nothing free about it in the Father's eye; it is all about getting even. And yet somehow, the Lamb's purity is such that he is not polluted by contact with the poisons he is loaded with.

There are thus gifts that though *from* our hands are really taken *off* our hands, either by people so low as to be untouchables, or so high as to be untouched by some special state that preserves them from being defiled by our toxic offerings.[9] Not surprisingly, in this understanding of the gift, the donor wishes to alienate his gift completely. Reciprocity is not looked for, nor desired. He gives not with a spirit of generosity, which he thus need not pretend to have, but from a combination of fear, interest, and duty. It is with regard to such toxic gifts to the gods that we are quite willing to regard their mere acceptance of our offerings as a more than sufficient return.[10]

The doctrine of the free gift, we see, has more than one dark side. Yet, as Audun indicated, for all my spoiling of its party, there is still some small space open for short durations in which a free gift of unarguably great and positive value, like some anti-matter, can exist before it quickly disappears.

The one kind of gift we know for certain raised no obligation to reciprocate was the closing gift. This gift was meant to end the cycle of exchanges. Though it itself could be a repayment, it could be in

---

[8] See Gloria Goodwin Raheja's *The Poison in the Gift: Ritual, Prestation, and the Dominant Caste in a North Indian Village* (Chicago, 1988); and see too Parry's insightful discussion of the same Indian evidence; "*The Gift*, the Indian Gift, and the 'Indian Gift'," pp. 459–461.

[9] The comparison may be somewhat forced but one could see Jesus playing both the role of untouchable as an enfleshed human, and the role of God, whose infinite resources allows his purity to survive the toxicity of our vileness.

[10] It is perhaps cheap to note that the high can turn their acceptance of this poison to their advantage, via burdens of guilt to be borne by the low, or by intercepting any complaint on the part of the low about their needless suffering by claiming greater suffering borne on their behalf.

such an amount that it more than requited any prior obligation and thus might have raised a new obligation to requite it, unless, that is, it were understood absolutely that it was final, that this was it.[11] Take Svein's final gift of the ring, and Harald's final gifts of a sword and cloak: they are not intended to elicit yet another return in an eternal cycle of gift exchange, much the way we get locked into never-ending cycles of email because we may feel that the last message still demands a response lest we be thought to be snubbing the other, when he or she is trying to indicate without offending that closure to the exchange is not only appropriate but also desperately wished for.

Svein's gifts to Audun are meant to send him on his way never to return, and likewise Harald's gifts of sword and cloak are parting gifts meant to close off the exchange cycle, that this tale is at an end. Final gifts can be insults to the extent they signal enough is enough, that dealings are now over, and surely not all final gifts are successful at bringing closure; sometimes people will not take a hint. Sometimes they leave behind their umbrella and will soon return to collect it; and then invite you out the next day for coffee. But the risk of glitch or an unwelcome reappearance is quite small when the recipient lives in another country a dangerous journey away.

Final gifts are also one of the prerogatives of kings, or of those of high standing, to give to, rather than to receive from, people of lower rank. The low do not give final gifts to the high. Here, take this seven-year-old ox and with it my blessings, sire; this is it, enough of your visits each year with a hundred retainers.[12]

There is another kind of closing gift, however, that is not final. In Iceland the sagas mention that hosts send their guests away with

---

[11] See C.A. Gregory's schema in which the countergift should exceed the gift it requites. The excess value is then understood to constitute a new gift that triggers a new repayment obligation; "Gifts to Men and Gifts to God." Value determination, though, for so many of the gifts exchanged was hardly an exact science. There was usually enough fuzziness in evaluation for people with reason to declare themselves adequately quit or grumble they had been shorted, or feel shamed they had been bested, by one and the same return gift.

[12] On this issue see the delicacy and political work that must be engaged in for humbler farmers to inform the district big man that his visits with his retinue are beyond their means; *Ófeigs þáttr* in *Ljósvetninga saga*, C version, chs. 6–7 (ÍF 10:115–121); trans. Theodore M. Andersson and William Ian Miller, *Law and Literature in Medieval Iceland*, pp. 139–144. See Algazi's account of the complex series of negotiations over rights of the lord to hospitality from a certain village in "Feigned Reciprocities: Lords, Peasants, and the Afterlife of Late Medieval Social Strategies," in Algazi et al., pp. 99–127.

unspecified "good gifts". These are meant only to bring closure to a particular occasion and are not final gifts in the sense Harald's and Svein's to Audun are final. These routine good gifts that the host gives to departing guests are meant to assure future interaction not to prevent it.[13] Closing gifts of both kinds can be divorced from specific requitals; they serve a different function than paying back a gift received.

A sword and a cloak given by a king are kingly gifts. They were real treasures, says the text, not mere tokens. They are not like spare change given to a beggar. They are not meant as a minimal good riddance. Harald's parting gifts are intended to do honor to Audun and bring the right kind of ritualized closure to their interactions. They thus must be of a quality to signal that this was a successful visit.

Audun returns to Iceland, proving himself to be the luckiest of men, and here his story ends by tracing his lineage to Thorstein Gyduson, the epilogue thus providing the story extension in time, as the prologue provided it in space from Iceland to Norway to Greenland and back to Norway. Audun produces real progeny, who are good men, one worthy of mention, but not sagaworthy; we know not much more about Thorstein Gyduson than that he was well-off and that he died by drowning.

Typical of these short tales, the wondrous, as we noted, happens abroad; back home reality sets in. Audun fathers offspring but his sagaworthiness is over. In Iceland, the criteria for what is worth telling are a bit different; the tales grow less tall on one dimension, but are more practically heroic on another. One critic, discussing the travel-abroad episodes that appear frequently in the sagas, notes the difference between the romance world of Icelanders abroad where they win fame and say No to kings and the all-too-real world at home of contention, feud, litigation, and killing.[14]

---

[13] Von Amira says these parting gifts are intended to signal that the friendship has survived the visit, given the ease with which these visits could turn into quarreling and discord; *Nordgermanisches Obligationenrecht*, 2:612–613. The routinization of these parting gifts can hardly bear such an interpretation, though perhaps in their darkest origins they bore such a meaning. The sagas, though, show more than a few feasts turning into fights. Thus the wry authorial comment regarding an offended guest leaving in a huff in *Þorgils saga ok Hafliða*, ch. 10: "it was not mentioned that he was given any gifts on parting."

[14] Geraldine Barnes, "Authors, Dead and Alive in Old Norse Fiction," *Parergon: Bulletin of the Australian and New Zealand Association for Medieval and Renaissance Studies*, NS 4 (1990), 5–22.

That is true of many who return from abroad in the sagas, which are longer prose forms; but *Audun's Story* is a *þáttr*, a short story, that ends, we can reasonably believe, because Audun had the good luck back home in Iceland to live out the rest of his life beneath the radar of sagaworthiness except for his one storied encounter with kings, which meant, presumably, and as his descendant Thorstein Gyduson's wealth attests, that he lived a relatively uncontentious life, husbanded his wealth well, and passed it on to his kin when he died. He probably counted it a blessing that his short story stayed pleasantly short and did not become a longer saga where he would be called on to defend his newly acquired wealth and honor, where the virtues he would need might include martial skills more than, or as well as, his head for business. A good part of Audun's good luck is that his story ended when it did.

There is this too: unlike most Icelanders who travel abroad and get recognized for their excellence by kings and magnates, Audun does not already come from an established family, nor is he a skald with a marketable talent that kings were willing to pay for. He can by virtue of coming from an undistinguished background have an easier time staying out of high-stakes competition for honor and power that is the stuff of the family sagas when he returns home.

Audun is true to the type in the sagas of the Icelander who comes home no matter how tempting the Sirens in the glamorous world abroad might be. Imagine how Henry James would have told this early version of an international story. Audun would have stayed on at Svein's court and, like some medieval Strether, would have become beguiled with the court and its life. James's Audun would "evolve", becoming more deeply self-conscious, more alienated from his origins, would abandon his mission and return home reluctantly, if at all. Audun is the opposite.[15] He throws himself fully into his adventures abroad, but they don't seem to change his psychology. He still has debts to pay, obligations to fulfill in Iceland, though now he has more than sufficient means to discharge them. And if Rome improves his soul, it doesn't affect his diction: he still says No to kings, and will now narrate the whole tale of his successful nay-saying back home to the delight of his countrymen in the same terse and witty style it has come down to us, parts of which tale, we saw, he had already been trying out on kings.

---

[15] Thanks to John Crigler for the James comparison.

CODA: THE WHITENESS OF THE BEAR

Ishmael's meditation on whiteness is among the most famous chapters that is not an opening chapter in English/American literature:

> What the white whale was to Ahab, has been hinted; what, at times, he was to me, as yet remains unsaid. Aside from those more obvious considerations touching Moby Dick, which could not but occasionally awaken in any man's soul some alarm, there was another thought, or rather vague, nameless horror concerning him, which at times by its intensity completely overpowered all the rest...It was the whiteness of the whale that above all things appalled me.

Thereupon follows a rhetorical tour of force that mobilizes myriad examples of whiteness to appall—from nature, religion, literature, physics, and metaphysics.

In fairness, and because he cannot deny it even if unfair, Ishmael concedes whiteness to have a good side; he lists its associations with royalty, sanctity, heavenly pomp, dominion of all sorts, some no longer credited to white's good side. Then comes the transitional adversative conjunction, "yet":

> yet for all these accumulated associations, with whatever is sweet, and honourable, and sublime, there yet lurks an elusive something in the innermost idea of this hue, which strikes more of panic to the soul than that redness which affrights in blood.

What occupies first position on whiteness's debit ledger? The polar bear.

> This elusive quality it is, which causes the thought of whiteness, when divorced from more kindly associations, and coupled with any object terrible in itself, to heighten that terror to the furthest bounds. Witness the white bear of the poles.

Ishmael then couples "the white bear of the poles" with the terror evoked by "the white shark of the tropics", which even in days before the book and film *Jaws* would appall on rather different grounds than a polar bear would. Before *Jaws* no one thought to comfort toddlers with teddy sharks or read them of Winnie the Shark.[1] White bears, no

[1] After *Jaws*, however, white shark cuddly toys appeared.

less than brown bears, are the stuff of stuffed cuddly toys that bring comfort to kids.

But Ishmael disagrees; the polar bear in his view is hideous, irresponsibly ferocious:

> With reference to the Polar bear, it may possibly be urged by him who would fain go still deeper into this matter, that it is not the whiteness, separately regarded, which heightens the intolerable hideousness of that brute; for, analysed, that heightened hideousness, it might be said, only rises from the circumstance, that the irresponsible ferociousness of the creature stands invested in the fleece of celestial innocence and love; and hence, by bringing together two such opposite emotions in our minds, the Polar bear frightens us with so unnatural a contrast. But even assuming all this to be true; yet, were it not for the whiteness, you would not have that intensified terror.

Ishmael would not dare to express such sentiments today in the west, with polar bears endangered, their ice floes melting beneath them so that they have no place to surprise the unlucky seal who surfaces for air at the wrong one of its severally maintained breathing holes. The seal now has plenty of open water, a good distance from the expectant bear, from which to surface to gulp its air. The bear goes as hungry now as Audun's did in Denmark. But then Ishmael's opinions on polar bears contrast no more starkly with ours than with those of this Icelandic tale. And though our sentimentalized views can be indulged safely via television or behind barriers imposed by zookeepers, Audun's could not. Audun's fright? None *from* his white bear and surely none on account of any eeriness felt to inhere in its whiteness; his worries were *for* his bear, that it might starve, that it might be confiscated by the "irresponsible ferociousness" of King Harald.

The bear's viciousness is not even suggested in the story unless we understand its peculiar red cheeks to have been incarnadined from messily slurping up seal blood. Its "intolerable hideousness" becomes in our tale its "exceptional beauty". We remarked very early in this book the nonchalance of the tale about the labors that must have occupied Audun caring for and transporting his bear until they both ran out of food. But more remarkable it would be to Ishmael, and to us too, is that in no version of *Audun's Story* is the bear's whiteness even mentioned. The sole color term applied to it occurs only in our manuscript (F), where the redness of its cheeks is noted to the bear's advantage, but not even this much colors the other versions in which its cheeks go unmentioned. The bear is called the bear, the animal, or the treasure.

Whiteness could have easily been invoked, with no effort, because the Old Icelandic term for polar bear, is "white bear" (*hvítabjörn*).[2]

If Ishmael (and certainly Melville) seeks for Symbol with a big S as an end in itself, our author studiously avoids symbolizing except in ways that he could deny if he were confronted with it: as with the trip to Rome and Audun's being bathed and arrayed in Svein's Lenten clothes (another suppressed and unmentioned white?). Whiteness does not move him, even to mention it. Yet what is special about the bear is indeed its whiteness, but not because that makes it unnerving or especially horrifying, not because it might suggest purity in holy matrimony with carnivorousness, as one might with Eucharistic associations, but because whiteness is what makes the bear rare, beautiful, and valuable.

Görsemi, "treasure," is the idea evoked by the unmentioned whiteness. And the word is used again and again, nine times in reference to the bear.[3] For it is *value* itself that the bear symbolizes, if it must symbolize anything. The whiteness makes it a treasure. The bear thus turns out to be a kind of money; and if anything must work as a symbol to work at all (beyond the banal observation that words work that way too) it is money, even when that money is also a sheep or a cow or cloth woven from wool. The whiteness of the bear makes it a value magnet that attracts kings, making the bear an especially appropriate gift to them which will be repaid with gifts that also qualify as a *görsemi*, loaded with symbolic value that a lowly Icelander can cash out, at least in part, once he gets home.

Any symbolizing that our author actually might have meant to evoke he couldn't avoid anyway. That symbolizing, as was detailed earlier, came from the philological evocativeness of the most basic words he needed to tell his tale. There is the play of the words for gift and luck, deriving from forms of the root "give". Then the ideas of gift and luck are semantically embedded in the first syllable of Audun's name, with its etymological origins in a root meaning fate, wealth, luck, woolen cloth, and weaving. And just as there was no way the author could avoid associations raised by the usual words for luck and gift in his tongue,

---

[2] The bear that Ingimund gave to King Harald Fairhair mentioned in *Landnámabók* is specifically called *hvítabjörn*; see above p. 18n8.

[3] Audun's bear is referred to as *bjarndýr* five times and simply as *dýr*, "animal" thirteen times; *görsemi*, in addition to referencing the bear, is also used once in reference to the ring Svein gives to Audun that is passed on to Harald, and once to describe the sword and cloak Harald gives to Audun as parting gifts.

he may have had the symbolic associations of Audun's name thrust upon him by fate of a different sort. Audun may in fact have been the name of Thorstein Gyduson's ancestor who established Thorstein's line as a wealthy one by giving a white bear to a king. Audun's making a name for himself thus brought with it certain subtle symbolic fortuities that our author, in a style that characterizes saga writing at its best, employed with reticence and unobtrusiveness. Audun is not the only lucky man; so, it seems, was the author.[4]

But the whiteness that makes this bear a value magnet is more than a matter of mere scarcity. Not all scarcity is *mere* scarcity; sometimes symbolism is hard to suppress. True, the whiteness of the bear cannot match the eeriness of the whiteness of Ahab's whale if it tried. Whiteness is natural to polar bears; it is what most identifies them as a species. But Moby Dick's whiteness makes him one of a kind and horrifying for being so singular. And he does not disappoint, for he lives up to the ominous reputation his whiteness vests him with.

Yet the unmentioned but crucial whiteness of Audun's bear touches in one small way on a specialness peculiar to its kind of scarcity, not so that it rises to the level of eeriness, but surely so that it transcends the usual in a way that prompts some awe. The bear's whiteness meant it came from the end of the world, in their sense of the world, for Greenland was, by the time of this tale's telling, the limit of the Norse world, the colony in North America having failed almost two centuries earlier. It thus took a sagaworthy effort to bring the bear to market, for it came from the outer limits. Might we thus see, with a little imagination, that the whiteness submerged in authorial silence, though there by necessary implication, is represented by the only other color term in the story: green. Its Greenlandic origin and its being a treasure are what prove that it is white without having to say so.

How uncanny the coincidence, though, that both *Moby Dick* and *Audun's Story* are tales of obsession; and both obsessions are inseparable from rareness conferred by whiteness on certain animals, one yielding tragedy, the other the best of all possible worlds. Both are tales of the sea in very different senses; in one the sea is central, in the other it is a practical necessity both economically and narratively. Both stories end sublimely in forms of exchange, one friendly, the other vengeful:

---

[4] Unless Thorstein Gyduson's enterprising ancestor's name was not Audun, but was given that name by the author precisely because of its symbolic associations.

Audun handing over the arm-ring to Harald and Tashtego pinning the unlucky sky-hawk to the mast with his hammer as the Pequod goes down "drag[ging] a living part of heaven along with her." The Viking tale is one of peace and good luck in wartime; the whaler's tale an all-consuming losing battle of and against cosmic forces in "peacetime." End with this stark contrast: one is dizzyingly fecund of words, the other so reticent, so understated, so chary of its words that it did not dare, or care, to name the color, let alone give that color its own chapter, that made the tale worth telling.

BIBLIOGRAPHY

Adam of Bremen. *History of the Archbishops of Hamburg-Bremen*. Trans. Francis J. Tschan, with new introduction and bibliography by Timothy Reuter. New York, 2002.

Æthelberht, Laws of. See Attenborough, ed., pp. 1–17.

Algazi, Gadi, Valentin Groebner and Bernhard Jussen, eds. *Negotiating the Gift: Pre-Modern Figurations of Exchange*. Veröffentlichungen des Max-Planck-Instituts für Geschichte, 188. Göttingen, 2003.

——. "Doing Things with Gifts." In Algazi et al., pp. 9–27.

——. "Feigned Reciprocities: Lords, Peasants, and the Afterlife of Late Medieval Social Strategies." In Algazi et al., pp. 99–127.

Andersson, Theodore M. *The Growth of the Medieval Icelandic Sagas, 1180–1280*. Ithaca, NY, 2006.

Andersson, Theodore M. and Kari Ellen Gade, introduction and trans. *Morkinskinna: The Earliest Icelandic Chronicle of the Norwegian Kings (1030–1157)*. Islandica 51. Ithaca, NY, 2000.

Andersson, Theodore M. and William Ian Miller. *Law and Literature in Medieval Iceland*. Stanford, 1989.

Anglo-Saxon Chronicle. http://asc.jebbo.co.uk/intro.html.

Appadurai, Arjun, ed. *The Social Life of Things: Commodities in Cultural Perspective*. Cambridge, 1986.

——. "Introduction: Commodities and the Politics of Value." In Appadurai, ed., pp. 3–63.

Arnold, John H. *Belief and Unbelief in Medieval Europe*. London, 2005.

Asu-Thord's story. ÍF 11:337–349. Trans. Andersson and Gade, pp. 330–334; CSI 3:442–346.

Attenborough, F.L., ed. and trans. *The Laws of the Earliest English Kings*. 1922. Rpt. New York, 1963.

Auðunar þáttr vestfirzka (M version). ÍF 6:359–368. Introductory matter: 6:c–cviii.

Bagge, Sverre. *The Political Thought of the* King's Mirror. Odense, 1987.

Barnes, Geraldine. "Authors, Dead and Alive in Old Norse Fiction." *Parergon: Bulletin of the Australian and New Zealand Association for Medieval and Renaissance Studies*, NS 4 (1990), 5–22.

Bartlett, Robert. *England under the Norman and Angevin Kings, 1075–1225*. Oxford, 2000.

Bishop Isleif's Story. See *Ísleifs þáttr byskups*.

Bjarnar saga Hítdælakappa. ÍF 3:109–211. Trans. CSI 1:255–304.

Bloch, Marc. *Feudal Society*. Trans. L.A. Manyon. Chicago, 1964.

Boulhosa, Patricia Pires. *Icelanders and the Kings of Norway: Mediaeval Sagas and Legal Texts*. Leiden, 2005.

Bourdieu, Pierre. *Outline of a Theory of Practice*. Trans. Richard Nice. Cambridge, 1977.

——. "Marginalia: Some Additional Notes on the Gift." In *The Logic of the Gift: Toward an Ethic of Generosity*. Ed. Alan D. Schrift. New York, 1997, pp. 231–41.

Brand the Generous's Story. Brands þáttr örvi. Trans. Andersson and Gade, pp. 219–220; CSI 1:374–375.

Caillé, Alain. *Don, intérêt et désintéressement: Bourdieu, Mauss, Platon et quelques autres*. Paris, 2005.

Calabresi, Guido and A. Douglas Melamed, "Property Rules, Liability Rules, and Inalienability: One View of the Cathedral." *Harvard Law Review* 85 (1972), 1089–1128.

Clover, Carol J. "Scene in Saga Composition." *Arkiv för Nordisk Filologi* 89 (1974), 57–83.

——. "The Long Prose Form." *Arkiv för Nordisk Filologi* 101 (1986), 10–39.

——. "Regardless of Sex: Men, Women, and Power in Early Northern Europe." *Speculum* 68 (1993), 363–388.

Cook, Robert. "On Translating Sagas." *Gripla* 13 (2002), 107–145.

CSI. *The Complete Sagas of Icelanders including 49 tales.* Ed. Viðar Hreinsson 5 vols. Various translators. Reykjavík, 1997.

de Vries, Jan. *Altnordisches Etymologisches Wörterbuch.* Leiden, 1961.

Egils saga. ÍF 2. Trans. CSI 1:33–177.

Elster, Jon. *Sour Grapes: Studies in the Subversion of Rationality.* Cambridge, 1983.

Eyrbyggja saga. ÍF 4:1–184. Trans. CSI 4:131–218.

F. See Flateyjarbók.

Fagrskinna. ÍF 29.

Fichtner, Edward G. "Gift Exchange and Initiation in the *Auðunar þáttr vestfirzka.*" *Scandinavian Studies* 51 (1979), 249–272.

Firth, Raymond. *Economics of the New Zealand Maori* 2nd ed. Wellington, NZ, 1959.

Flateyjarbók. *Flateyjarbók: en samling af norske konge-sagaer med indskudte mindre fortællinger om begivenheder i og udenfor Norge samt annaler.* 3 vols. Ed. Guðbrandur Vigfússon and C.R. Unger. Christiania [Oslo], 1860–1868.

Fóstbræðra saga. ÍF 6:119–276. Trans. CSI 2:329–402.

Frank, Roberta. "Viking Atrocity and Skaldic Verse: The Rite of the Blood-Eagle." *English Historical Review*, 99 (1984), 332–343.

Freud, Sigmund. "The Antithetical Meaning of Primal Words." 1910. *Standard Edition* 11:153–162.

Frostaþing Law. See NGL.

Gade, Kari Ellen. "Homosexuality and Rape of Males in Old Norse Law and Literature." *Scandinavian Studies* 58 (1986), 124–141.

——. "Einarr þambarskelfir's Last Shot." *Scandinavian Studies* 67 (1995), 153–162.

Gautreks saga. In Fornaldarsögur Norðurlanda 4:1–50. See *Gift-Ref's Saga.*

Geary, Patrick. "Sacred Commodities: The Circulation of Medieval Relics." In Appadurai, ed., pp. 169–191.

Gelsinger, Bruce E. *Icelandic Enterprise: Commerce and Economy in the Middle Ages.* Columbia, SC, 1981.

Gift-Ref's Saga. Gjafa-Refs saga. In Fornaldarsögur Norðurlanda. Ed. Guðni Jónsson. Reykjavík, 1954. 4 vols. 4:36–50. Trans. Hermann Pálsson and Paul Edwards, *Gautrek's Saga and other medieval tales.* New York, 1968, pp. 43–53, chs. 9–11 of *Gautreks saga.*

Gilbert, Anthony J. "Social and National Identity in some Icelandic *þættir.*" *Neophilologus* 75 (1991), 408–424.

Ginzburg, Louis. *The Legends of the Jews.* 6 vols. Baltimore, 1953; rpt. 1998.

Goffman, Erving. *The Presentation of Self in Everyday Life.* New York, 1959.

Gordon, E.V. *An Introduction to Old Norse.* 2nd ed. Rev. A.R. Taylor. Oxford, 1957.

Gouldner, Alvin W. "The Norm of Reciprocity: A Preliminary Statement." *American Sociological Review* 25 (1960), 161–178.

Graeber, David. *Toward an Anthropological Theory of Value: The False Coin of our own Desire.* New York, 2001.

Grágás: Islændernes lovbog i fristatens tid. 3 vols. Ed. Vilhjálmur Finsen. Copenhagen,1852 (Konungsbók), 1879 (Staðarhólsbók), 1883. Rpt. Odense, 1974. Translation of Konungsbók with selections from Staðarhólsbók and other mss, see: *Laws of Early Iceland: Grágás. The Codex Regius of Grágás with Material from other Manuscripts.* 2 vols. Trans. Andrew Dennis, Peter Foote, and Richard Perkins. Winnipeg, 1980, 2000. Vol. 1 contains *Grágás* Ia 1–Ia 217; vol. 2, *Grágás* Ia 218–Ib 218 in Finsen's pagination.

Gregory, C.A. "Gifts to Men and Gifts to God: Gift Exchange and Capital Accumulation in Contemporary Papua." *Man* 15 (1980), 626–652.

——. *Gifts and Commodities*. London, 1982.
Guðmundar saga Arasonar. In Byskupa sögur. Ed. Guðni Jónsson. Reykjavík, 1953. 2:167–389.
Guðmundar saga dýra. In *Sturlunga saga* 1:160–212. Trans. McGrew and Thomas, 2:145–206.
Guéry, Alain. "Le roi dépensier: le don, la contrainte et l'origine du système financier de la monarchie française d'Ancien Régime." *Annales ESC* 39 (1984), 1241–1269.
Gulaþing Law. See NGL.
Gurevich, A.Y. "Wealth and Gift-Bestowal among the Ancient Scandinavians." *Scandinavica* 7 (1968), 126–38.
——. *Medieval Popular Culture: Problems of Belief and Perception*. Trans. János M. Bak and Paul A. Hollingsworth. Cambridge, 1988.
H. See Hulda.
Halldor's Story. *Halldórs þáttr Snorrasonar II*. ÍF 5:263–277. Trans. Hermann Pálsson, *Hrafnkel's Saga and other Stories*, pp. 94–108; Andersson and Gade, pp. 187–194; CSI 5:223–230.
Hallfreðar saga. ÍF 8:133–200. Trans. CSI 1:225–253.
Harris, Joseph C. "Genre and Narrative Structure in some *Íslendinga Þættir*." *Scandinavian Studies* 44 (1972), 1–27.
——. "Theme and Genre in some *Íslendinga Þættir*." *Scandinavian Studies* 484 (1976), 1–28.
Hávamál. In *Edda: die Lieder des Codex Regius*. 3rd ed. Hans Kuhn. Heidelberg, 1962, pp. 17–44. Trans. Carolyne Larrington, *The Poetic Edda*. Oxford, 1996, pp. 14–38.
Heimskringla. Vol. 1: *Óláfs saga Tryggvasonar*. ÍF 26:225–372; Vol. 3: *Haralds saga Sigurðarsonar*. ÍF 28:68–202; Trans. Magnus Magnusson, *King Harald's Saga*. Harmondsworth, 1976.
Herzog, Don. "Externalities and other Parasites." *University of Chicago Law Review* 67 (2000), 895–924.
Heusler, Andreas. *Altisländisches Elementarbuch*. 4th ed. Heidelberg, 1950.
Holt, J.C. "What's in a Name? Family Nomenclature and the Norman Conquest." In Holt, *Colonial England 1066–1215*. London, 1997, pp. 179–196.
Hreidar the Fool's Story. *Hreiðars þáttr*. ÍF 10:245–260. Trans. Hermann Pálsson, *Hrafnkel's Saga and other Stories*, pp. 109–120; Andersson and Gade, pp. 171–179; CSI 1:375–384.
Hudson, John. *Land, Law, and Lordship in Anglo-Norman England*. Oxford, 1994.
——. *The Formation of the English Common Law: Law and Society in England from the Norman Conquest to Magna Carta*. London, 1996.
Hulda. H version of *Audun's Story*. In Fornmanna Sögur. Ed. Sveinbjörn Egilsson, et al. 12 vols. Copenhagen, 1825–1837. 6:297–307.
Hungrvaka. ÍF 16:1–43. Trans. Gudbrand Vigfusson and F. York Powell, *Origines Islandicae*. 2 vols. Oxford, 1905. 1:425–458.
ÍF. *Íslenzk Fornrit*. Reykjavík:
ÍF 1. *Landnámabók*. Ed. Jakob Benedicktsson. 1968.
ÍF 2. *Egils saga Skalla-Grímssonar*. Ed. Sigurður Nordal. 1933.
ÍF 3. *Borgfirðinga sögur*. Ed. Sigurður Nordal and Guðni Jónsson. 1938.
ÍF 4. *Eyrbyggja saga*. Ed. Einar Ól. Sveinsson and Matthías Þórðarson. 1935.
ÍF 5. *Laxdæla saga*. Ed. Einar Ól. Sveinsson. 1934.
ÍF 6. *Vestfirðinga sögur*. Ed. Björn K. Þórólfsson and Guðni Jónsson. 1943.
ÍF 8. *Vatnsdæla saga*. Ed. Einar Ól. Sveinsson. 1939.
ÍF 9. *Eyfirðinga sögur*. Ed. Jonas Kristjánsson. 1956.
ÍF 10. *Ljósvetninga saga*. Ed. Björn Sigfússon. 1940.
ÍF 11. *Austfirðinga sögur*. Ed. Jón Jóhannesson. 1950.
ÍF 12. *Brennu-Njáls saga*. Ed. Einar Ól. Sveinsson. 1954.
ÍF 16. *Biskupa sögur*. Vol. 2. Ed. Ásdís Egilsdóttir. 2002.

ÍF 26–28. *Heimskringla*. 3rd ed. Ed. Bjarni Aðalbjarnarson. 1979.
ÍF 29. Fagrskinna. Haralds saga Ed. Bjarni Einarsson. 1985.
Ísleifs þáttr byskups. Bishop Isleif's Story. ÍF 16:335–336.
Íslendinga saga. In *Sturlunga saga* 1:229–534. Trans. McGrew and Thomas, *The Saga of the Icelanders*. 1:115–447.
Jaeger, C. Stephen. *The Origins of Courtliness: Civilizing Trends and the Formation of Courtly Ideals, 939–1210*. Philadelphia, 1985.
Jewish Study Bible. Ed. Adele Berlin and Marc Zvi Brettler. Oxford, 2004.
Jones, Gwyn, trans. *Eirik the Red and other Icelandic Sagas*. Oxford, 1961. *Audun and the Bear*, pp. 163–170.
Jussen, Bernhard. "Religious Discourses of the Gift in the Middle Ages: Semantic Evidences (Second to Twelfth Centuries)." In Algazi et al., pp. 173–192.
Kochen, Madeline. *The Divine Lien*. Forthcoming.
Konungsannáll. In *Annálar og Nafnaskrá*. Ed. Guðni Jónsson. Reykjavík, 1953, pp. 1–74.
Konungs skuggsiá. Ed. Ludvig Holm-Olsen. Oslo, 1945. Trans. Laurence M. Larson, *The King's Mirror*. 1917. Rpt. New York, 1972.
Kopytoff, Igor. "The Cultural Biography of Things: Commoditization as Process." In Appadurai, ed., pp. 64–94.
Koziol, Geoffrey. *Begging Pardon and Favor: Ritual and Political Order in Early Medieval France*. Ithaca, NY, 1992.
Kreutzer, Gert. "Von Isländern, Eisbären, und Königen: Anmerkungen zur Audun-Novelle." *Trajekt* 5 (1985), 100–108.
Kuchenbuch, Ludolf. "Porcus donativus: Language Use and Gifting in Seigniorial Records between the Eighth and the Twelfth Centuries." In Algazi et al., pp. 193–246.
Landnámabók. ÍF 1. Trans. Hermann Pálsson and Paul Edwards, *The Book of Settlements*. Winnipeg, 1972.
La Rochefoucauld, *Maxims*. Trans. Leonard Tancock. Harmondsworth, 1959.
Larson, Laurence M. ed. and trans. *The Earliest Norwegian Laws, being the Gulathing Law and the Frostathing Law*. New York, 1935.
Laxdæla saga. ÍF 5. Trans. Magnus Magnusson and Hermann Pálsson. Harmondsworth, 1969; CSI 5:1–120.
Leges Henrici Primi. Ed. and trans. L.J. Downer. Oxford, 1972.
Lichtheim, Miriam, trans. and ed. *Ancient Egyptian Literature* vol. 2: *The Middle Kingdom*. Berkeley, 1976.
Lincoln, Bruce. *Theorizing Myth: Narrative, Ideology, and Scholarship*. Chicago, 1999.
Lindow, John. "Old Icelandic *þáttr*: Early Usage and Semantic History." *Scripta Islandica* 29 (1978), 3–44.
Ljósvetninga saga. ÍF 10:1–139. Trans. Anderson and Miller.
Louis-Jensen, Jonna. *Kongesagastudier*, Bibliotheca Arnamagnæana 32. Copenhagen, 1977.
M. See Morkinskinna.
Macaulay, Thomas. "Mill's Essay on Government." In *The Miscellaneous Writings of Lord Macaulay. 2 vols. London, 1860*, pp. 282–322. Original in *Edinburgh Review*, 1829.
Mani the Poet's Story. *Mána þáttr skalds*. Trans. CSI 1:339.
Mauss, Marcel. *The Gift*. Trans. W.D. Halls. New York, 1990.
Maxwell, Anthony. *The Tale of Audun from the West Fjords*. CSI 1:369–374.
McGrew, Julia H. and R. George Thomas, trans. *Sturlunga saga*. 2 vols. New York, 1970–74.
Meulengracht Sørensen, Preben. *The Unmanly Man: Concepts of Sexual Defamation in Early Northern Society*. Trans. Joan Turville-Petre. Odense, 1983.
Middle Assyrian Laws. See Roth, Martha T.
Miller, William Ian. *Bloodtaking and Peacemaking: Feud, Law, and Society in Saga Iceland*. Chicago, 1990.

——. *Humiliation: and other essays on Honor, Social Discomfort, and Violence*. Ithaca, NY, 1993.
——. *Faking It*. Cambridge, 2003.
——. "Home and Homelessness in the Middle of Nowhere." In Nicholas Howe, ed. *Home and Homelessness in the Medieval and Renaissance World*. South Bend, IN, pp. 125–42.
——. *Eye for an Eye*. Cambridge, 2006.
Morkinskinna. Ed. Finnur Jónsson. Samfund til udgivelse af gammel nordisk literatur, 53. Copenhagen, 1932. Trans. with critical discussion see Andersson and Gade.
NGL. *Norges gamle Love indtil 1387* 5 vols. Vol. 1: *Norges love ældre end Kong Magnus Haakonssöns regjeringstid fra 1263 til 1280*. Ed. R. Keyser and P.A. Munch. Christiania [Oslo], 1846. Trans. Larson. *The Earliest Norwegian Laws*.
Nimis, Stephen A. "Ring Composition and Linearity in Homer." In *Signs of Orality: The Oral Tradition and Its Influence in the Greek and Roman World*. Ed. E. Anne Mackay. Leiden, 1998, pp. 65–78.
Njáls saga. ÍF 12. Trans. Magnus Magnusson and Hermann Pálsson. Harmondsworth, 1960.
Óláfs saga Tryggvasonar. ÍF 26.
Pálsson, Hermann. *Hrafnkel's Saga and Other Stories*. Harmondsworth, 1971.
Parry, Jonathan. "*The Gift*, the Indian Gift, and the 'Indian Gift'." *Man* 21 (1986), 453–473.
Pokorny, Julius. *Indogermanisches Etymologisches Wörterbuch* 4th ed. Tübingen, 2002.
Ragnarssonar þáttr. In Fornaldarsögur Norðurlanda. Ed. Guðni Jónsson. Reykjavík, 1954. 1:287–303.
Raheja, Gloria Goodwin. *The Poison in the Gift: Ritual, Prestation, and the Dominant Caste in a North Indian Village*. Chicago, 1988.
Ranisch, Wilhelm, ed. *Die Gautrekssaga in zwei Fassungen*. Palaestra, XI. Berlin, 1900.
Raphals, Lisa. "Fate, Fortune, Chance and Luck in Chinese and Greek: A Comparative Semantic History," *Philosophy East & West* 53 (2003), 537–74.
Regesta Regum Anglo-Normannorum: The Acta of William I (1066–1087). Ed. David Bates. Oxford, 1998.
Roth, Martha T., ed. and trans., *Law Collections from Mesopotamia and Asia Minor*. Atlanta, GA, 1995.
Rowe, Elizabeth Ashman. "Cultural Paternity in the Flateyjarbók *Óláfs saga Tryggvasonar*." *Alvíssmál* 8 (1998), 3–28.
S.-Christen, Eliana Magnani. "Transforming Things and Persons: The Gift *pro anima* in the Eleventh and Twelfth Centuries." In Algazi et al., pp. 269–284.
S. Gregorii Magni Registrum Epistularum. Ed. Dag Norberg. Turnholt, 1982.
Sahlins, Marshall. *Stone Age Economics*. Chicago, 1972.
Sarcastic-Halli's Story. *Sneglu-Halla þáttr*. ÍF 9:261–295 (M and F versions). Trans. CSI 1:342–357 (F version); Anderson and Gade, pp. 243–252 (M version).
Saxo Grammaticus. Danorum regum heroumque historia: bks x–xvi. 3 vols. Trans. and commentary, Eric Christiansen. British Archaeological Reports International Series. Oxford, 1980.
Sayers, William. "The Honor of Guðlaugr Snorrason and Einarr þambarskelfir: A Reply." *Scandinavian Studies* 67 (1995), 536–544.
Schelling, Thomas C. *The Strategy of Conflict*. Cambridge, 1960.
Sneglu-Halla þáttr. See *Sarcastic-Halli's Story*.
Sørensen. See Meulengracht Sørensen.
Spufford, Peter. *Money and its use in Medieval Europe*. Cambridge, 1988.
Stirling, Ian. *Polar Bears*. Ann Arbor, MI, 1988.
Stuf's Story. *Stúfs þáttr*. ÍF 5:279–290. Trans. Andersson and Gade, pp. 255–257; CSI 1:357–359.

Sturlu saga. In *Sturlunga saga* 1:63–114. Trans. McGrew and Thomas, *The Saga of Hvamm-Sturla*. 1:59–113.
Sturlunga saga. Ed. Jón Jóhannesson, Magnús Finnbogason, and Kristján Eldjárn. 2 vols. Reykjavík, 1946.
Sverris saga. In *Konunga sögur* vol. 2. Ed. Guðni Jónsson. Reykjavík, 1957. Trans. J. Sephton, *The Saga of King Sverri of Norway*. London, 1899.
Sweet, Henry. *An Icelandic Primer with Grammar, Notes and Glossary*. Oxford, 1886.
Taylor, Arnold R. "Auðunn and the Bear." *Saga-Book of the Viking Society* 13 (1946–53), 78–96. Trans. at pp. 81–87.
Thorarin Short-Cloak's Story. *Þorarins þáttr stuttfelda*. Trans. Anderson and Gade, pp. 347–349; CSI 1:360–361.
Thorgrim Hallason's Story. *Þorgríms þáttr Hallasonar*. ÍF 9:297–303. Trans. CSI 3:467–470.
Thorstein from the East Fjords' Story. *Þorsteins þáttr austfirðings*. ÍF 11:327–332. Trans. CSI 1:390.
Thorvard Crowbeak's Story. *Þorvarðar þáttr krákunefs*. ÍF 6:369–374. Trans. Andersson and Gade, pp. 223–225; CSI 1:397–399.
van Caenegem, R.C., ed. *English Lawsuits from William I to Richard I*. 2 vols. London, 1990–1991.
van Wees, Hans. "Reciprocity in Anthropological Theory." In *Reciprocity in Ancient Greece*. Ed. Christopher Gill, Norman Postlethwaite and Richard Seaford. Oxford, 1998, pp. 13–50.
Vápnfirðinga saga. ÍF 11:21–65. Trans. CSI 4:313–334.
Vatnsdæla saga. ÍF 8:1–131. Trans. CSI 4:1–66.
Vita S. Eligii, Life of Saint Eloi. In J.-P. Migne, *Patrologia Latina*. http://pld.chadwyck.co.uk/. Vol. 87, col. 533C.
Vlastos, Gregory. "Equality and Justice in Early Greek Cosmologies." *Classical Philology* 42 (1947), 156–178.
von Amira, Karl. *Nordgermanisches Obligationenrecht*. 2nd vol. *Westnordisches Obligationenrcht*. Leipzig, 1895.
Wagner-Hasel, Beate. "Egoistic Exchange and Altruistic Gift: On the Roots of Marcel Mauss' Theory of the Gift." In Algazi et al., pp. 141–171.
Watkins, Calvert. "New Parameters in Historical Linguistics, Philology, and Culture History." *Language* 65 (1989), 783–799.
Weber, Gerd Wolfgang. *Wyrd: Studien zum Schicksalsbegriff der altenglischen und altnordischen Literature*. Bad Homburg, 1969.
Weiner, Annette B. *Inalienable Possessions: The Paradox of Keeping-While-Giving*. Berkeley, 1992.
White, Stephen D. "Service for Fiefs and Fiefs for Service: The Politics of Reciprocity." In Algazi et al., pp. 63–98.
Þorgils saga ok Hafliða. Ed. Ursula Brown. London, 1952. Trans. McGrew and Thomas, *The Saga of Thorgils and Hafliði*. 2:25–70.
Þorvarðar þáttr krákunefs. See *Thorvard Crowbeak's Story*.

INDEX

www.ingramcontent.com/pod-product-compliance
Ingram Content Group UK Ltd.
Pitfield, Milton Keynes, MK11 3LW, UK
UKHW050953290926
15470UKWH00006B/1795

9 789004 168114